Computing in Musicology

An International Directory of Applications

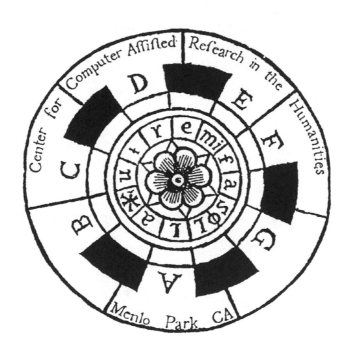

Center for Computer Assisted Research in the Humanities
Menlo Park, CA

Volume 9   **1993-4**

ISBN 0-936943-08-4
ISSN 1057-9478

Printed by Thomson-Shore, Inc., of Dexter, MI

for the

Center for Computer Assisted Research in the Humanities
525 Middlefield Road, Suite 120
Menlo Park, CA 94025-3443
XB.CAR@Forsythe.Stanford.Edu or *XB.CAR@Stanford.Bitnet*

Preface

This volume of *Computing in Musicology* shows departures of several kinds from previous issues. It includes two sections on new topics—an exposition on the Center's own work in the development of *MuseData* databases and the first controlled survey anywhere of software for optical recognition of music. It also includes the results of our first reader survey on software preferences. The notation software section emphasizes very recent music. Some articles on tools and applications are more detailed than those we have published in previous years. All of these items bear witness to the evolution of the field.

Here at CCARH we have been developing fully encoded versions of eighteenth- and early-nineteenth-century musical repertories for almost ten years. While we usually refrain from featuring our own work in *Computing in Musicology*, we made an exception this year in order both to accommodate the many questions that we receive about our activities and to describe a timely topic.

Tom Mathiesen's article on document preparation and delivery was commissioned to anchor a section on the still vexing problem of integrating musical information with text information in single documents. Yo Tomita's description of a tool for inserting musical information into database, spreadsheet, and word-processing software complements Matheson's article.   Shorter articles on online resources attest to the growing opportunities for quick, easy retrieval of valuable information and resources.   The divergent approaches of José Bowen and Guerino Mazzola to studies of tempo form a complementary pair.   John Morehen's report on a database of fingering patterns in Elizabethan keyboard music is a model of systematic procedure related to a practical concern.

As a developing field, software for optical recognition of music stands roughly where software for music notation stood ten years ago—in various labs (principally academic ones) awaiting sufficient enhancement to permit the emergence of serviceable commercial programs. The recent appearance of two commercial programs and one that is available by FTP urged us to look closely at this technically challenging activity. We are not sure that the questions we asked were the most vital or revealing, but we appreciate the advice provided by Nicholas Carter, one of the young pioneers in this field and a frequent contributor to *CM*, who was in residence at the Center in 1992-3, and the responses provided by those developers who were brave enough to reply.

We would like to acknowledge our special gratitude to Ann Basart, director of Fallen Leaf Press in Berkeley, California, and to the composers whose works are represented in this issue for authorizing the use of these excerpts, which come from the Press's publication *Fallen Leaves* (1992). Contemporary works have been poorly represented in previous issues because of the difficulties usually involved in obtaining the requisite permissions from copyright holders.

Our survey of user applications involving sound, notation, and analysis software, which was distributed in the summer of 1993, elicited just over 350 responses. We wish to thank these respondents not only for the stock answers but also for the bounty of free-form information they provided. We expect that many readers who did not respond will find the results enlightening.

We have eliminated altogether the news section on the grounds that most information is available more quickly by electronic means. However, we will continue to include important publications in the "Further Readings" section.

We would especially like to acknowledge the help of Frances Bennion, Edmund Correia, Jr., Steven Rasmussen, Nancy Solomon, and R. Clive Field for their timely and diligent assistance in assembling, preparing, and proofreading the materials in this issue.

Menlo Park, CA
February 2, 1994

Contents

A List of Tables

Data

The *MuseData* Universe:

A System of Musical Information

The *MuseData* Universe:
A System of Musical Information

MuseData is a large body of comprehensively encoded standard repertory. Acting as the hub of a group of music codes, this repository is designed to support applications involving sound, notation, and analytical tasks.

MuseData has been under systematic development for almost ten years at the Center for Computer Assisted Research in the Humanities in Menlo Park, CA, entirely in its own code with non-commercial programs for data input, storage, and management. The *MuseData* system of musical data management differs from other systems in its aim of serving as a master set of information from which subsets can be extracted to support multiple kinds of applications. *MuseData* is not tailored to any particular piece of software or any particular computer platform. The intention is to provide encodings that are comprehensive for diverse applications and complete in their support for any one of them. Versatility is provided by translation from the *MuseData* representation to a range of application-specific codes.

Conversion of musical information from one code to another is a complex process that forces many choices. Its originators view *MuseData* as the sun of a solar system in which applications program codes are the satellites. *MuseData* illuminates the entire range of music applications and facilitates rapidly increased and improved use of existing applications software. Depending on the perspectives from which we view them, the satellite formats supported have their own strengths, cast their own shadows, and form diverse constellations.

This commentary describes (1) the solar system—components and principles of data organization, (2) the planets—attributes of selected satellite formats, (3) the sun—features of *MuseData* that provide a basis for translation to these formats, and (4) the effects of planetary motion—attributes of post-translation hybrid formats. The system design and all supporting programs have been created by Walter B. Hewlett.

---

* *MuseData* and *MIDI+* are trademarks of the Center for Computer Assisted Research in the Humanities.

The System:
Components and Principles of Organization

Tracks, Parts, and Scores

To accommodate diverse needs, *MuseData* consists of three kinds of files—track files, part files, and score files. Track and part information sets are synonymous in many kinds of music (*e.g.*, a string quartet). One example of a place in which they are different is a keyboard fugue: there is only one part (for keyboard), but in order to analyze the fugue it is necessary to know what is happening in each track (voice). Similarly, there are many cases in which part and score files will contain information that differs only in the organization. However, to encourage full utilization of the information it is essential to recognize the possibility of divergence. Cue notes in an instrumental part offer a good example of "score" information that is required in a part. Even simple things like dynamics signs must be displayed once for every part in part files and suppressed in most parts in a score file. Multi-bar rests offer another familiar case in which the needs of the part (one indicator) are graphically different from the needs of the score (a rest in a series of bars).

To accommodate the highly varied means of musical organization in existing software, *MuseData* files are translated to a number of special-purpose formats for sound, notation, and analysis.

Musical Sources and Editions

It has always been the intention of CCARH to provide encodings based on the best available musical sources. Modern editions already in print are generally not useable for reasons of copyright. CCARH selects its sources from the collected editions made chiefly in the nineteenth century and from original source materials, such as composer's autograph manuscripts, copies made under the supervision of the composer, and prints of earlier centuries, chiefly the eighteenth. Occasionally CCARH commissions new editions of old works. This has especially been the case with our current Handel holdings, which include recent editions of several oratorios (*Susanna*, *Messiah*, *Judas Maccabaeus*), operas (*Ottone*, *Radamisto*, *Poro*), and serenatas (*Tirsi, Clori, e Fileno*). CCARH has also collaborated with the Telemann Zentrum in Magdeburg, Germany, in creating performance materials for previously unedited works, such as *Teutschland grünt und blüht im Friede* (1989) and *Orpheus* (1990).

By creating scores and parts for performance by professional groups (notably, in the case of Handel, for Philharmonia Baroque Orchestra and the Göttingen Handel Festival), the system used to convert stored data to useable performance materials has been well tested. These newly created editions also make available rereadings, reorchestrations, and supplementary material provided by widely recognized specialists including Nicholas

McGegan, John Roberts, Anthony Hicks, Terence Best, Mark Stahura, Peter Huth, and Wolfgang Hirschmann as well as corrections supplied after performances by participating musicians.

The Input Process

MuseData files are created by a highly skilled staff using materials recommended by various bodies of music scholars and professional performers. Information concerning pitch and duration is captured in a first phase. MIDI keyboards are used but the MIDI file format is not used to record or store information. A syntax-checker receives all the initial data and calls attention to obvious errors. An interpreter supplies the enharmonic information not available from MIDI input. These track files are printed and proofread. At a later stage part files are assembled into short and full scores for proof-hearing.

In a second stage, the files are reformatted and information that cannot be provided by keyboard is added alphanumerically. Text underlay for vocal music and information representing slurs, dynamics, articulations, and so forth are supplied at this stage.

Multiple Representations

The key to supporting applications in both sound and graphics is often to provide a double representation for situations in which there is a discrepancy between the logic of musical notation and the logic of sound. In the case of a *da capo* aria (ABA), for example, data for printing will terminate with the final bar of the B section. Data for sound output will normally recapitulate the A section after the completion of the B section. Separate indicators are required to suit these dual purposes.

Another conflict between printing and sound is that of transposing parts. Print-based codes represent the part at written pitch. Sound-based codes represent it at concert pitch. *MuseData* provides a part file at each of the pitches, for although automatic transposition is easy to accomplish if sound output is the only thing desired, print programs often stumble over the need for some inversions of stem directions and beam placements as well as collisions with text underlay and the consequent possibility of needing to reallocate the overall spacing of staves within a system.

Records are also added to facilitate the realization of natural-sounding ornaments in sound applications. Here again, a printing application requires that a quarter note with an ornament be printed as a quarter note, whereas a performance giving the quarter note full weight and omitting the ornament sounds unrealistic. Conversely, an encoding that gives solely a written realization of the reduced-value quarter note that is complemented by a real-time ornament cannot adequately support notation, for the values will appear to be erratic.

Data requirements for musical analysis vary greatly with the task at hand. For many traditional kinds of analysis sound information is preferable to graphic information. This is especially true of studies involving accent and many aspects of rhythm. Many kinds of analysis require some kind of extrapolation from the input code, for example from a pitch string to a melodic contour or from the detail of a melodic surface to the simplicity of a Schenkerian *Urlinie*. Programs to facilitate such adaptations are likely to be written by users in the years ahead.

The Planets:
Attributes of Selected Satellite Formats

On the basis of a years-long study of music representation issues and the results of the survey conducted during the summer of 1993, CCARH selected as the initial satellite codes for *MuseData* files *DARMS*, *SCORE*, MIDI, and *Kern*. Other formats are also under consideration.

DARMS and *SCORE* are the most complete codes for representing notated music. Although the codes themselves are system-independent, the existing commercial software that uses these codes runs on PCs under DOS. Windows versions of *The Note Processor* (using *DARMS*) and *SCORE* are soon to be released.

At the present time there is no Macintosh notation software which possesses an open code and is in widespread use. This situation is related to the use of the graphical user interface. GUIs are not designed to rely on logical-symbolic information. Recognizing the restrictions that the GUI imposes on import and export capabilities, *Nightingale* has developed a metacode called *Notelist*. Recognizing the limitations of a closed code, Coda Music Technology has promised to publish the *Enigma* file format used by *Finale*—when the next version (4) is released. This may not happen soon, since version 3 has only come to market within recent months.

Notational Information in *DARMS*, *SCORE*, and *MuseData*

There is an important practical difference between *DARMS* and *SCORE*. *DARMS* builds scores up from parts. Thus the primary files are encodings of single parts. In *The Note Processor*, page layout issues are resolved in the program after the data has been acquired. In *SCORE* the assembled score is the core of the work. The primary files represent single pages of the score, described from the lowest part in the bottommost system to the highest part in the topmost system. *MuseData* part files serve as the basis for translations to *DARMS*; *MuseData* score files serve as the basis for translations to the *SCORE* format.

DARMS and *SCORE* have the common strength of providing very articulate information for printing. A great many parameters that are not captured in MIDI data are captured in *DARMS* and *SCORE*. The *Note Processor* can accept MIDI files and there is a third-party program to enable *SCORE* to do the same thing. The inevitable result of using MIDI programs as a basis for notation is that vis-à-vis the strength of codes such as *DARMS* and *SCORE*, the user suffers an enormous sacrifice of information necessary for printing that MIDI was not designed to provide. Output to MIDI is a simpler matter, since it involves going from more to less, but even here there can be some misrepresentation of information, since *DARMS* and *SCORE* are entirely tied to notation.

Scores and parts can be printed from *MuseData* files using *MuseData* notation software, which runs within the *TenX* environment on PCs. At the present time, this software is not available to the public.

Sound Information in MIDI, *MuseData* and Alternative Sound Codes
MIDI

MIDI needs no introduction as the predominant code currently in use for sequencers. Since it originated as a hardware interface, MIDI is highly machine oriented and quite unfriendly to casual users. Because it has been so heavily used since it was first devised in 1986, MIDI has also been revised and extended in numerous ways. Myriad adaptations threaten to cause some fragmentation of the body of code associated with the Standard MIDI file.

While there is no doubt that MIDI serves its intended purpose of generating sound on a keyboard synthesizer well, its foundation in sound imposes serious limitations on its value as a file format for generating notation. Almost all of the information added to CCARH files in the second stage of input is unrepresentable in MIDI files. There is also some attrition of first-stage data. Examples follow.

Enharmonic pitches (C♯ and D♭ share a common pitch number) cannot be specified. As a practical matter, MIDI file displays may arbitrarily indicate all accidentals as sharps (or flats), since the pitch name is superfluous to the functioning of the hardware interface.

MIDI does not strictly indicate durations. It merely indicates when particular note numbers turn on and off. It does not therefore represent rests per se, only elapsed time between one note-off and an ensuing note-on. This is just one of several rhythmic liabilities that may be encountered when one attempts to generate sensible notation from a MIDI file.

Although there are schemes for representing certain kinds of performance information, such as dynamic level (code-named "velocity" in MIDI parlance), in MIDI files, these features are often ignored in MIDI files and may not be treated uniformly from program to program.

Articulation indications become especially problematical in the MIDI environment when one attempts to support both sound and notation. Staccatos, for example, must be turned off substantially before the next note is turned on. The printed version of the realized staccato will, however, generate rests that would not appear in an ordinary print. In this respect, the time information in MIDI is too literal to match the fuzzy logic of written music. Some notation programs that have grown up with MIDI data (one example that comes to mind is *Encore*) deal with this problem by giving full value to the stored duration and implementing the articulation on the fly, according to specifications provided interactively by the user.

An articulation problem of more recent vintage is that of tremolos. Under General MIDI specifications of instruments, the violin tremolo is a separate instrument from the violin. If one has a Standard MIDI file that represents the part of a violin in an ensemble, tremolo indications within the part will not be realized in performance unless the "instrument" is switched. If the tremolos are occasional rather than continuous, it is impractical to attempt to realize them electronically.

Alternative Sound Codes

Alternative sound codes do exist. One of them is *Csound*, a favorite in the Unix community. By virtue of being a sound code, *Csound* has many of the deficits of MIDI, but the code is more transparent and the acoustical results are better suited to the trained ear. There is no translation of *Csound* to a format supporting notation. Analysts working with *Csound* are concerned with analysis of sound, not of notated music.

Translations of *MuseData* to MIDI include extensions that facilitate correct interpretation of enharmonic pitches for notational purposes. A translation of *MuseData* to *Csound* is being written independently.

MuseData

The native format of *MuseData* has merit as a basis for some kinds of sound applications. *MuseData* sound records provide humanly intelligent, non-mechanical realizations of ornaments that some users may prefer to formulaic MIDI implementations of trills and turns. Because these sound records co-exist with notation records, output to notation programs does not produce the durational distortions that occur when MIDI input containing realized ornaments is used.

MuseData files have been adapted to work with Max Mathews's *Radio Baton*, which facilitates the conducting of selected parts in a rehearsal environment and full scores in an electronic performance environment.

Analytical Information in *DARMS*, *SCORE*, MIDI, *Kern*, and *MuseData*

Until recently analysts were disinclined to distinguish between score-based analysis and sound-based analysis. They were assumed to be equivalent. Electronic music has changed the picture dramatically. The small ways in which sound and score vary can have a significant effect on results achieved through machine manipulation of data. Pitch representation is one of the most familiar examples.

DARMS

Since *DARMS* was designed purely for music printing, it equated pitch with a vertical position on a staff. It does not use pitch names or octave names. In the manner of modern scores, it does not restate an accidental within the bar. However, if one wanted to count all the B♭s in a *DARMS* file one would have to track several variables (clef, beat count, etc.) to locate them.

SCORE

SCORE is a cleaner code for this purpose, since it gives pitch names, even if it does not restate accidentals within the bar. In *SCORE*, however, pitch and duration are recorded in separate tracks, so while *SCORE* code is adequate for searching for specific pitch patterns or duration patterns, it is less well suited to searching for pitch-and-duration patterns. *SCORE* input code does not distinguish between a tie and slur (on the grounds that they are drawn in the same general way), so detailed durational searches would be difficult to conduct in repertories having a lot of ties.

Significant quantities of information required for printing are lost when *MuseData* is translated to *SCORE* input code. Because the main strength of *SCORE* is in the extent of its capabilities for music printing, the translation supported by *MuseData* is to *SCORE* parametric tables. Although these can be used for analytical tasks, they are less well suited to the task than the input code.

MIDI

While MIDI data may be adequate for certain kinds of analysis (especially those that are indifferent to tonality and precise rhythmic information), its value will vary considerably with circumstances. Unquantized data (that is "performances") are all but useless for any query that involves duration. The fancy spectrograms that have been a staple of many sequencer programs are inherently interesting in picturing sound processes and may serve a useful purpose in various educational settings, but they have little to offer the experienced researcher.

Kern

    Kern is a code designed to facilitate analysis. It is not yet in widespread use, although it is familiar to a number of researchers involved in studies of music perception and cognition. It is one member of a family of codes that work with analysis tools in the *Humdrum* kit. The fact that *Kern* does not provide a basis for musical notation enables it to be better suited to many kinds of analytical tasks than *DARMS* and *SCORE*. *Kern* is extremely flexible. There is no specific number of attributes that must be encoded with *Kern*. It will store a text underlay or a string of articulations without necessarily including the associated pitches. Since *Kern* has been used for the study of non-Western repertories of highly diverse sorts, it is difficult to make general statements about it. *Kern* files for classical music of multiple parts are organized in a score format whereby the lowest part is represented by the leftmost column. As in the *Note Processor*, a *Humdrum* program is available to assemble *Kern* scores from parts. *MuseData* files in the *Kern* format are made from *MuseData* score files.

MuseData

    MuseData's native format is undoubtedly of considerable value for many analytical tasks. Since it provides, when necessary, separate descriptions of sound and graphical information, it should be especially useful for enquiries that pertain to these differences (*notes inégales* and other Baroque rhythmic practices, for example).

    Analytical applications of *MuseData* for the Macintosh are under development at the University of California at Santa Cruz by David Cope, David Evan Jones, and others. *MuseData* files have also provided raw material for the style lexicons used in Cope's *Experiments in Musical Intelligence*, which are directed toward the creation of artificial repertories in the styles of designated composers.

    MuseData files are currently in use in a range of investigations led by psychologists Carol Krumhansl (Cornell University) and Caroline Palmer (The Ohio State University). Krumhansl's work includes efforts to test the implication-realization model of melodic expectation conceived by Eugene Narmour. Palmer's work is concerned with performance errors and measurements of expression.

    MuseData files are also in use in acoustical research by Eckhard Kahle at IRCAM in Paris. Diverse other uses have been made of encodings of the *Well-Tempered Clavier* that have been on deposit in the Oxford Text Archive since 1986.

The Sun: A Source for
Translatable Musical Information

Since the format in which *MuseData* files exist was conceived as one capable of supporting applications of diverse sorts, the primary focus has been on preserving the logic of musical concepts as expressed both in written notation and in performance. Among these, however, there are many contradictions. In their emphasis on graphic objects, code-based music printing programs may introduce concepts whose meaning is purely graphical. *DARMS*, for example, treats pitch as vertical placement on a staff. *SCORE* is somewhat ambiguous in its representation of ties and slurs.

Sound codes, similarly, are tailored to specific purposes. The MIDI note number 61 is not inherently C♯4 or D♭4; it is merely the frequency generated by the note lying between 60 (C4) and 62 (D4). Under General MIDI, pizzicato is treated not as a kind of articulation or an implication for duration but as an instrument species (*e.g.*, pizzicato strings). When MIDI data is imported into a printing program, the interpretation of accidentals, which is unimportant in the equal-tempered world of synthesizers, is entirely arbitrary.

The printed score as a representation of a sound process is itself imperfect and incomplete. There is no overriding logic to the whole of notation, nor is there complete consensus on the verbal (much less the numerical) description of sound. If there were, then new performances of known works would serve no fulfilling purpose; two reviews of the same concert or recording would be identical.

One Note, Many Attributes

The representation of music in multiple formats is a subject too complex to be fully explored here. Two fundamental concepts can, however, be appreciated. One is the idea that one note (notation) or event (sound) has many attributes. See Figure 1.

Not all attributes are represented in every code. If they were, there would probably not be as many codes as there are. Most codes were developed for one specific purpose, which is well served. Problems arise when codes devised for one purpose are put to use for another. Pitch (or some substitute for it) and duration are the most basic attributes. The number of other attributes is indeterminate. Some systems of music representation make provision for as many as 64 attributes for each note.

The other important concept is that elements of information that are treated as data attributes in one system may be computationally derived in another. The need for stems, flags, beams, and durational dots that are each counted as separate attributes in *DARMS*, for example, are usually generated automatically from interpreting a single durational value in programs written over the past several years. Yet automatic computations are never infallible, and for complex music a good result may be more rapidly achieved from a precise encoding than from a graphically emended image.

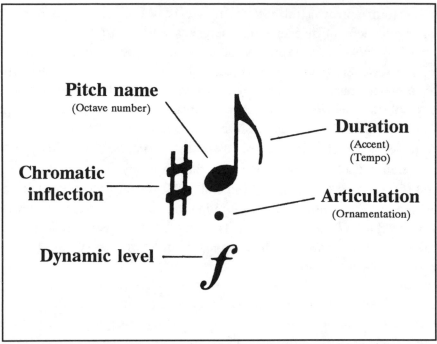

Figure 1. A note and its attributes. Most attributes named in bold type are deducible from the information present. Pitch cannot be interpreted without a staff and clef. Attributes named in lighter type, which are not represented here, require more contextual cues for interpretation.

Some problems in this class are quite subtle. The playing techniques of staccato, pizzicato, and vibrato offer some good examples.

• *Staccato* playing has the actual effect of reducing durations without reducing the time that elapses between beats. If durations are reduced in MIDI data that is used to generate musical notation, superfluous rests between notes will often be generated.

Several programs that play MIDI data assume staccato notes to be presented in their full durations. Users are given tools to implement MIDI at various levels of reduction.

- *Pizzicato* playing also has the actual effect of reducing durations, but it is achieving by plucking rather than by bowing and its timbral quality is therefore slightly different. General MIDI, a commonly agreed upon set of "instrument numbers" that produce the same timbral quality on any piece of hardware, treats pizzicato strings as a separate "instrument" from bowed strings. Not only can pizzicato not be represented durationally for use in MIDI applications, but a single string part with a pizzicato passage can only be accurately reproduced in a General MIDI environment by treating its bowing changes as instrument changes.

- *Vibrato*, a playing or singing technique producing a slight fluctuation in pitch, is not normally represented in scores but it is ubiquitously present, under user control, on electronic instruments. It is hypothetically a performance attribute that is ignored in notation.

The accommodation of key elements used in representing music by these various systems in their native condition is summarized in Tables 1 through 4.

Element	MuseData	DARMS	SCORE	MIDI	Kern
Pitch name	explicit for every note	can be derived from clef	explicit for every note	not given	explicit for every note
Octave number (parameter)	absolute for every note	can be derived from clef	relative to initial octave code; can be reset	can usually be derived from note number	absolute for every note
Octave number (nomenclature)	Middle C = C4	none	Middle C = C4	Middle C = 60[1]	Middle C = C4
Chromatic inflection	explicit for every note	appropriate signs supported	appropriate signs supported	not given	explicit for every note

Table 1. Attributes related to notated pitch.

---

[1] Most software programs decode "60" as C4 but a few decode it as C3.

Elements	MuseData	DARMS	SCORE	MIDI	Kern
Rests	explicit	explicit	explicit	not represented	explicit
Ties	explicit	explicit	defined as graphic occurring *between* two notes	total duration correct but object not represented	explicit
Slurs	explicit	explicit	defined as graphic occurring above/below two or more notes[2]	not represented	explicit; distinct slur, phrase markings
Nested slurs	explicit	explicit	explicit	not represented	explicit[3]
Stems	explicit[4]	explicit[4]	automatic, with override[4]	not represented	not encoded
Stem direction	explicit	explicit	automatic, with override	not represented	explicit[4]
Beams	explicit	explicit	automatic, with override	not represented	explicit
Tuplets (unusual note subdivisions)	supported	supported	supported	supported	supported
Fermatas	explicit	explicit	explicit	not represented	explicit

Table 2. Attributes related to notated duration.

---

[2] Some *SCORE* users prefer the appearance of the slur to that of the tie and use this graphic in both cases. This can give rise to ambiguity in files.

[3] *Kern* also supports elisions (instances in which a new slur begins before an active slur has ended). Phrases and slurs can be marked so that the beginnings and endings are explicitly matched, as illustrated by the following structure:

```
    (        (        )        (        )        )
    1        2        1        3        3        2
```

[4] In *MuseData*, *DARMS*, and *SCORE*, input codes for stems and stem directions are normally set by default. The user can override these defaults. In *DARMS*, *SCORE*, and *Kern*, noteless stems and stemless noteheads are supported.

Element	MuseData	DARMS	SCORE	MIDI	Kern
staccato	symbol supported	symbol supported	symbol supported	symbol not supported; effect can be realized	symbol supported
detached legato	symbols supported	symbols supported	symbols supported	symbol not supported; effect can be realized	symbols supported
tenuto	symbol supported	symbol supported	symbol supported	symbol not supported	symbol supported
pizzicato	verbal instruction and MIDI instrument change supported	treated as verbal instruction	treated as verbal instruction	treated as separate instrument	treated as verbal instruction
measured (bowed) tremolo [single pitch; abbreviated notation]	individual notes represented separately	treated as symbol(s) or individual notes	generally treated as symbol(s)	symbol(s) not supported; individual notes can be reiterated	individual notes represented separately
fingered tremolo [alternating pitches; abbreviated notation]	individual notes represented separately	treated as symbol(s) or individual notes	generally treated as symbol(s)	treated as separate instrument	symbol supported

Table 3. Selected attributes of articulation.

Effects of Planetary Motion:
Attributes of Post-Translation Hybrid Formats

These differing conceptions of what music is—a printed score, a set of parts, a sound stream, a structured collection of data for analytical use make some kinds of translation more practical and complete than others.

In details of file organization, *MuseData* part files, *DARMS* part files, and Standard MIDI Format 1 (one track per channel) files form one constellation, in which the basic organizing element is the single part. *MuseData* score files, *SCORE* internal files, and *Kern* files form another constellation, in which the complete texture of the work is taken as the fundamental element.

Even within these general divisions, there are daunting differences. *DARMS* has the capability of including multiple parts—let us say all the parts of a string quartet—in one file for situations in which only a score is desired. MIDI has channel constrictions: hypothetically a maximum of 16 parts can be assigned, but this number can be diminished by copyright notices, percussion tracks, and other impositions made by software. When the number of data tracks is greater than the number of available channels, the solution that makes the best musical sense is to consolidate instruments of like timbre (*e.g.*, Horn 1 and Horn 2) on one channel. Effectively this means integrating MIDI Format 0 (all tracks on one channel) information in a MIDI Format 1 environment.

As for the score-oriented formats, *SCORE*'s file structure is page-oriented, while *Kern*, being uninvolved with notation, represents a steady stream of data.

Hybrid Formats

For such reasons, the species of *DARMS*, *SCORE*, *MIDI*, and *Kern* that *MuseData* supports are necessarily slightly hybridized. Where each system provides latitude, we must adopt one proven path of performance.

The ways in which *MuseData* translations to *DARMS*, *SCORE*, *MIDI*, and *Kern* differ from the native formats described are summarized below:

> *MuseData DARMS* provides a translation to the dialect used by the one printing program that works with *DARMS* code—*The Note Processor*. This dialect does not inhibit analytical uses, since it differs mainly from the original *DARMS76* [the 1976 version] in its treatment of beams. *DARMS* has been used more widely for short musical examples, such as incipits, and short compositions than for full scores. We find that, correspondingly, the program is most reliable for short works and works with only a few parts. It is therefore our current plan to offer *DARMS* translations only for works of six or fewer parts.

> *MuseData SCORE* files are translations to *SCORE*'s parametric intermediate files. These are tables of numbers that indicate precise placement for printing and are markedly different from the input files in which information concerning pitch, duration, and other features appear in separate strings. The advantage of translating to the parametric format is that very little information stored by *MuseData* is lost. In other words, the attempt is to support the highest quality of notation in a program known for its industrial-strength dependability and professional quality output.

Element	MuseData	DARMS	SCORE	MIDI	Kern
Tempo words	supported	supported	supported	metronomic control[5]	supported
Text underlay	supported via special characters [é, ñ, ö, à, etc.] represented by ASCII 1-128	supported (*NP*) via special characters represented by ASCII 129-256 = "Norwegian" set	supported via special characters represented by *PostScript* octal codes unique to *SCORE*	supported as time-stamped lyrics[5]; no provision for special characters	may be independently encoded
Ornaments	symbols and realization supported	symbols supported	symbols supported	symbols not supported	symbols supported
Fingering numbers	supported	supported	supported	not supported	may be independently encoded
Basso continuo figures	symbols attached to appropriate time slices	symbols in own track	symbols arbitrarily placed	symbols not supported	may be independently encoded
Binary repeats	symbols and appropriate repetition supported	symbols supported	symbols supported	symbols not supported; repetition may be transcribed	symbols supported
Alternative (first, second) endings	symbols and realization supported	symbols supported	symbols supported	symbols not supported; realization may be transcribed	symbols supported
Recapitulation schemes (da capo, minuet, *et al.*)	symbols and realization supported	symbols supported	symbols supported	symbols not supported	symbols supported
Alternative readings	supported by remarks attached to events in file	may be indicated as separate voice(s)	may be indicated through layout	not supported	may be independently encoded

Table 4. Other performance information.

[5] MIDI provides not only for time-stamped "lyric" meta-events (FF05) but also for other words to be incorporated into a "text" meta-event (FF01). The status of both is "optional," however; most notation programs and many sequencers do not recognize such events.

MuseData MIDI files support the main features of Standard MIDI Format 1 files and are not enhanced for performance. *MuseData MIDI+* files provide recapitulations, realization of ornaments, carefully selected instrumentations, and other accommodations to provide aesthetically pleasing music instead of a mere information stream. While the specifications of General MIDI are supported in both cases, some timbral selections are, for aesthetic reasons, different from the instrument names in printed parts. Users are, of course, welcome to make their own revisions.

MuseData MIDI+ files also contain extensions to facilitate more accurate notational recording of pitch information.

MIDI files generated from *DARMS* code and from *SCORE* code via the program *MIDISCOR*, a third-party product that works with *SCORE*, may lack some of these special features, since some performance attributes interfere with optimum printing.

MuseData Kern files provide a secure foundation for analytical use with *Humdrum* software. Because *Kern* is one subset of features intended specifically for analysis, certain visual attributes of a score may be absent.

The Score vs. The Music

The overriding difference between *MuseData* and other representation schemes is that, when necessary, *MuseData* provides dual encodings to produce accuracy in both notation (that is, the score) and sound (that is, the music).

A trill sign can be supported with one character, whereas the specific notes used to play a trill are multiple and may have different durations among the set. A trill realization, therefore, must be supported with a series of characters. Similarly, an abbreviation for a repeated note sequence may be adequately represented by a single symbol in a score but a musical performance requires information about each of the notes so represented.

Music scholars make a further distinction—between the current edition and the original work. To meet scholarly needs, corrections made in data entry and alternative readings are supported in footnotes within the file and attached to the appropriate events, so that a *MuseData* master file conforms, as nearly as possible, to standards of academic editions of music as they evolved over the past century.

In contrast to representations for notation only, in which placement of such information as basso continuo figures is correct as long as it achieves the proper vertical alignment, *MuseData* attaches all such information to events (or, when appropriate, to precise points between events). This facilitates accurate analysis of such details as text underlay, ornamentation, harmonic realization, and so forth in relation to pitch and duration.

Our hope is that *MuseData* will be complete enough to remove a large number of potential obstacles from the path of future data users. The most serious obstacle to date, however, has been a paucity of reliably encoded data. This situation should change dramatically as *MuseData* files become available for release.

Currently Encoded Works

At this writing, all of the following works have been encoded in the *MuseData* format:

- **J. S. Bach**: all major orchestral works; *St. Matthew Passion*; *St. John Passion* (two versions); *B-Minor Mass*; several dozen cantatas; many keyboard works (*Two- and Three-Part Inventions, Well-Tempered Clavier, Goldberg Variations, Art of Fugue*).

- **Beethoven**: three symphonies (Nos. 3, 5, 6); one piano concerto (No. 2); several quartets.

- **Corelli**: all (48) trio sonatas (Opp. 1-4); all (12) violin sonatas (Op. 5, two versions); all (12) concerti grossi (Op. 6).

- **Handel**: chamber sonatas Opp. 2 and 5; concertos Opp. 3 and 6; concertos for two orchestras; orchestral suites—*Water Music, Fireworks Music*; oratorios (*Messiah, Judas Maccabaeus, Susannah*), operas (*Ottone, Radamisto, Poro*); serenatas (*Tirsi, Clori, e Fileno*).

- **Haydn**: 56 string quartets; six symphonies (Nos. 1, 22, 31, 40, 99, 102).

- **Legrenzi**: trio sonatas (Op. 2; 18 works).

- **Mozart**: all string duos, divertimenti, (24) quartets, and (6) quintets; six symphonies (Nos. 35, 36, 38, 39, 40, 41); four horn concertos.

- **Schubert**: several works for string ensemble.

- **Telemann**: one opera, one serenata; 12 sonatas for flute and basso continuo; 84 sacred cantatas; *Tafel=Musik*.

- **Vivaldi**: concertos Op. 3 ("L'Estro Armonico"; 12 works) and Op. 8 (12 works including the "Four Seasons").

Translation programs to other formats (by Walter B. Hewlett, Brent A. Field, and others) are being debugged, and as these programs become serviceable, works are being translated to each respective code. The translated works are then reverified in the new code. Methods of distribution are under negotiation.

The author wishes to acknowledge with gratitude the important contributions of Tim Crawford, J. Stephen Dydo, Walter B. Hewlett, David Huron, and Leland Smith.

CCARH welcomes enquiries about *MuseData*.   These may be directed to Nancy Solomon, Center for Computer Assisted Research in the Humanities, 525 Middlefield Road, Ste. 120, Menlo Park, CA 94025-3443; tel.: (800) JSB-MUSE; fax: (415) 329-8365; e-mail: *XB.CAR@Forsythe. Stanford.Edu*. *Humdrum* music analysis software, which works with the *Kern* code, will shortly be available through CCARH.

Appendix:
An Overview of *MuseData* Files and Record Types

A CCARH file is organized as a set of variable-length records. Each file describes the music in one musical part of a musical work. A musical part may consist of one or more lines of music. Music on the grand staff may be considered as one or two parts.

A file has three sections—the header, the body of musical data, and an optional section for footnote data.

The Header

Header records 1-9 provide identifying information concerning the encoding process, the musical work, and the source(s) on which the encoding is based. These are currently assigned as follows:

Record 1: < *date* >   < *encoder* >
Record 2: free
Record 3: free
Record 4: WK#: < *work number* > MV#: < *movement number* >
Record 5: < *source* >
Record 6: < *work title* >
Record 7: < *movement title* >
Record 8: < *name of part* >
Record 9: free [may indicate < *mode* > and < *movement type* >]

Records 10 and 11 indicate relationships between this and other parts of the work. The format is

Record 10: Group memberships: < *name1* > < *name2* > . . .
Record 11: < *name1* >: part < *n* > of < *number in group* >
Record 12: < *name2* >: part < *n* > of < *number in group* > . . .

The Body

The body of a file follows directly after the header. With the exception of records between comment designator flags, all records in the body are data records. The order of these records is an integral part of the information contained in the file. The first character in each data record functions as a control code, describing the type of information contained in the record. For certain data types, such as notes, the first character also contains data information. This system of describing record types with a control code allows for significant future expansion of the file format. Currently there are 21 control codes and 12 data types.

DATA TYPES

1. **musical attributes**: key, divisions per quarter note, time designation, clef, staff, directives
2. **musical directions**: tempo indications, rehearsal numbers, pedal indications, crescendos and diminuendos, dynamics expressed by letters, octave transpositions, etc.
3. **bar lines** (controlling and non-controlling; single, double, dotted, etc.)
4. **regular notes and rests**: pitch name, octave number, chromatic inflection, duration; associated information about stems, beams, ties, slurs, ornaments, articulations, playing position
5. **extra note**(s) in a regular chord: same information as in #4, linked with a #4 event
6. **grace and cue notes**: same information as in #4, plus information about visual presentation; linked with a #4 event
7. **extra grace or cue notes** in a chord: same as #6; linked with a #6 event
8. **figured harmony**: figures, figure positions, visual presentation information
9. **forward or back space in time**: used to express parallel action within one part
10. **continuation line marker**
11. **comments**: a toggle to turn comment mode on and off
12. **end-of-music end-of-file marker**

Footnote Data

The optional footnote section begins after the final record of the main section. A footnote flag may be set for any attribute in the "regular notes" and related data types. Extended notes may be given in comment mode.

The encoding scheme also makes provision for levels of authority. This facilitates distinction between the content of the source(s) used, correction of probable errors, alterations suggested by possible errors, and so forth.

Encoding

The codes used to represent this information are somewhat arbitrary. They have been chosen for representing common musical notation for Western music from the sixteenth through the nineteenth centuries. The encoding scheme is not complete but may be augmented and/or altered to meet the special requirements of the music being encoded.

A draft manual is available from CCARH.

Document Delivery

The *TML* Model

CANTUS

The Chanson

Beethoven Bibliography

MRIS

Music Theory Online

Other Resources

Transmitting Text and Graphics in Online Databases: The *Thesaurus Musicarum Latinarum* Model

The application of computer technology to the development of machine-readable literary texts has been going on for many years, but the particular accomplishments of the *Thesaurus Linguae Graecae* (*TLG;* based at UC Irvine), the Center for Computer Analysis of Texts (CCAT; based in the Department of Religious Studies at the University of Pennsylvania), and the Packard Humanities Institute (PHI; in Los Altos, CA) provided the model for a similar sort of database to serve both the rather special needs of historians of music theory and the more general needs of cultural and intellectual historians, lexicographers, historians of science, and medievalists.

As readers of this periodical know, the *Thesaurus Musicarum Latinarum* (*TML*) is an evolving database that will eventually contain the entire corpus of Latin music theory written during the Middle Ages and the early Renaissance,[1] thereby facilitating the study of terminology, the identification of parallel passages or unattributed quotations, and the preparation of new critical editions. This in turn should assist scholars in developing a more comprehensive view of Latin music theory and, on a broader level, the intellectual history of the Middle Ages.[2]

---

[1] Coverage in the *TML* will extend from approximately the end of the fourth century (beginning with the *De musica* of Augustine and Book IX of Martianus Capella's *De nuptiis Philologiae et Mercurii*) to the end of the sixteenth century. Previous descriptions of the *TML* have appeared in *Computing in Musicology* 6 (1990), 133; 7 (1991), 37-39; and 8 (1992), 18-20, 40, 44, and 57-60. Classical Latin writings through 200 A.D. (and Biblical texts in several ancient languages) are available by licence on PHI CD-ROM 5.3. Further information is available from Brigitte Comparini, PHI, 300 Second Street, Los Altos, CA 94022; tel.: (415) 948-0150; fax: 948-5793; e-mail: *XB.MO7@STANFORD.BITNET.*

[2] The *TLG*, which was founded in 1972 and has been offering material on CD-ROM since 1986, has the task of controlling over 60,000,000 words; it concentrates entirely on published Greek texts and, in general, does not need to deal with graphic material such as musical notation, charts, and diagrams. The currently available "D" disk contains Greek literature through 600 A.D. Further information is available from Theodore Brunner, Director, Thesaurus Linguae Graecae, UC Irvine, Irvine, CA 92717; also William A. Johnson, same address; e-mail: *wjohnson@uci.edu.*

Data Delivery Models

A database such as the *TML* must be able to control both text and graphic material. Morevoer, because many Latin music treatises have not been published in critical texts, it needs to include the contents of manuscripts as well as published material. With more than 2,200,000 words of text currently online, the *TML* already makes it possible to locate and display in a matter of minutes every occurrence of a particular term, a phrase or passage, or a group of terms in close proximity in the treatises of more than 100 separate authors, several of them in multiple published editions and some manuscript sources.

Any database intended for public use should be widely available, easy to access, and structured to suit its material, its anticipated uses, and its mode of storage and delivery. It is therefore obvious that no one model can be presented for every database. Even text databases such as the *TML* and the *TLG* that are similar in type of material and anticipated uses differ considerably in the way in which the text is entered, indexed, delivered, and displayed. Differences in mode of storage and delivery, differences in the type or mechanism of searching and display, and differences in anticipated use need to be taken into account when designing the optimum structure for the material—the data—itself. In the case of a continuously growing database such as the *TLG*, which currently provides 60,000,000 words in fixed form on a compact disc, the mode of delivery has already been defined to a very great extent.[3] The *TLG*'s particular encoding requires specially designed programs to search and display the Greek text, but there are several alternatives that can be used on DOS or Macintosh machines, as well as on a special computer, the Ibycus Scholarly Computer, which was designed to facilitate use of this database. By contrast, a text database such as the Dartmouth Dante Project (DDP) is not delivered as a whole but queried from remote sites; the text files can therefore be structured to suit the single defined mechanism of searching, *BRS/SEARCH*.

There is currently no comparable resource for Latin literature. The *Thesaurus Linguae Latinae* (*TLL*) and the *Lexicon Musicum Latinum* (*LML*), both centered in Munich, are lexical databases; that is, they are arranged so that one can retrieve passages that illustrate the use of a particular word, but text strings and proximate text groupings cannot be searched nor can larger blocks of text be retrieved. Neither the *TLL* nor the *LML* are available online; the *TLL* is currently being published in individual fascicles and the files of the *LML* can be consulted on location in Munich.

[3] Although the database is not truly "delivered" until the CD is read in some way by the user's individual computer, the structure of the CD will largely predetermine the way in which it will be read. "Mode of delivery" refers to the way in which the database is made available to whatever search or display engines will be applied to it, not the actual manipulation of the database by these engines.

The *TML* differs from both of these projects in its flexibility and fluidity. Although the whole database resides on a single computer, it cannot be queried on this mainframe,[4] and no version of it is available to the public in a fixed form such as a compact disc. In order for the database to be used, it must first be delivered over the networks—Internet or Bitnet[5]—to a mainframe on which an individual has an account. It can then either be manipulated by various mainframe programs for searching and displaying text and graphics or it can be downloaded to any personal computer on which the text and graphics can be searched and displayed. In its mode of delivery, the *TML* is similar to various "electronic journals" such as the *Bryn Mawr Classical Review* or *Music Theory Online*. Electronic journals are themselves machine-readable text databases, but unlike the *TLG*, *TML*, or DDP, their data is intended to be used in large blocks—"articles" in the traditional parlance of printed journals.[6]

Any text database delivered on the networks must be structured in certain ways if it is to be securely transmitted. Here too, differences in anticipated use will affect the structure. For example, if a text database is to contain elaborate formatting or special characters that can only be displayed by a certain program, running perhaps on only a few types of machines, the data should certainly be encoded to insure use of only the relatively few types of characters likely to pass unmolested through all network gateways. If the data is to be encoded, it must be decodable by the person receiving it. There are a variety of schemes, some of which also involve data compression, but it is not such an easy matter to be sure that the decoding tables at every possible point of exit will match the one used for the original encoding.[7] On the other hand, if the text database is to be as universal as possible, so that it can be searched and displayed on any machine running a wide variety of programs, the text may not need to be encoded. It will still need to be specially structured. If the database includes graphics, as the *TML* does, these too will require special handling.

---

[4] Except to request the names and sources of available files.

[5] For further information on the networks and available network resources, see the excellent introduction "Using Networks in Musical Research" in *Computing in Musicology* 8 (1992), 33-54.

[6] The best introduction to many of the issues surrounding electronic texts, whether conceived as databases, full-text retrievals, or online journals, is *CD ROM, II: Optical Publishing: A Practical Approach to Developing CD ROM Applications*, ed. Suzanne Ropiequet with John Einberger and Bill Zoellick (Redmond, WA: Microsoft Press, 1987).

[7] UUencoding programs, for instance, which are relatively common on mainframes and also exist in versions for computers using DOS or the Macintosh operating system, are not universally compatible. Moreover, some UUencoding tables use ASCII 32, the space, as one of the possible characters, and this character may be filtered out or changed by some mainframe mailers. Sometimes the coding tables themselves are different from program to program, sometimes the filename created by one may not be acceptable to another, and so on.

The *TML* was envisioned from the start as a database that should be accessible on any computer, and after considerable practical experimentation at various test sites, the *TML* developed a system for structuring text and graphics enabling them to be securely transmitted over Internet and Bitnet and then to be searched and displayed on essentially any computer running any word processing or searching programs. This system is certainly not the only possible one, but it is a system that has now been tested and successfully operated for nearly three years.[8] A number of individuals developing online text databases have asked for information about the *TML*'s system, and it therefore seems appropriate to describe the system for a wider audience in the following paragraphs.

Text Files: Character Sets

It is a fixed principle of the *TML* that its text should be able to be displayed and searched on machines and operating systems ranging from CMS and VMS at one extreme to DOS and Macintosh at the other. All of these machines and their various programs, however, handle the interpretation of character sets (and display fonts) in different ways. This presents a considerable obstacle to the practical realization of the principle. In practical terms, only 95 characters are displayed consistently across the various platforms; these are commonly known as the standard or basic ASCII character set, ranging from ASCII 32, the space, to ASCII 126, the ~ :[9]

ASCII 32–47		!	"	#	$	%	&	'	(	)	*	+	,	-	.	/
ASCII 48–63	0	1	2	3	4	5	6	7	8	9	:	;	<	=	>	?
ASCII 64–79	@	A	B	C	D	E	F	G	H	I	J	K	L	M	N	O
ASCII 80–95	P	Q	R	S	T	U	V	W	X	Y	Z	[	\	]	^	_
ASCII 96–111	`	a	b	c	d	e	f	g	h	i	j	k	l	m	n	o
ASCII 112–26	p	q	r	s	t	u	v	w	x	y	z	{	|	}	~	

---

[8] The importance of practical experimentation cannot be too strongly emphasized. Assertions are regularly made about the stability and uniformity of various file transfer protocols, mailing systems, and similar resources allowing mainframes to communicate with each other on Bitnet and Internet. In fact, however, individual systems and network gateways have marked idiosyncrasies, and a method of transferring data that works perfectly between one set of sites may not work at all in some other combination of sites.

[9] I am ignoring here the relationship between ASCII (American Standard Code for Information Interchange) and EBCDIC (Extended Binary Coded Decimal Interchange Code), a coding system used primarily on IBM mainframes and minicomputers. Inasmuch as the delivery systems and retrieval software normally take care of the necessary translations back and forth, the relationship between ASCII and EBCDIC is not an important issue, except in the use of square brackets, which do not exist in EBCDIC.

ASCII numbers extend beyond 126, but no standard exists for the assignment of characters to the extended ASCII set. For example, the particular code (ASCII 213) that displays a curled apostrophe (') in one program (*Word*) on one machine may very well display an Old English lowercase eth (ð) in another program (*WordPerfect*) on some other machine. For all intents and purposes, only the standard character set can be confidently used in unencoded text transferred over the networks.

ASCII characters 1 through 31 support various control codes, including such things as linefeeds, returns, tabs, bells, cursor-key movement, and the like. Although these codes are relatively standard in their interpretation across various machines, even they are subject to some variation or modification. In the process of moving across the network, tabs, for instance, may be preserved or converted into a certain number of spaces, linefeeds may be filtered out or passed through, and so on.

Text making use of the standard ASCII character set can be printed, of course, but this is peripheral to the TML as a database. Basic ASCII text would certainly not have been the optimum structure for the texts had they been intended primarily or exclusively for viewing and printing rather than for viewing and searching. Here again, the intended use of the data affected decisions about its structure and delivery.

All these factors preclude in the *TML* font distinctions (such as italics, boldface, underlining, or non-Roman fonts), formatting that extends beyond vertical and horizontal alignment produced by the introduction of spaces or blank lines (in other words, a sort of "typewriter alignment"), and the use of diacritical marks or other special symbols. Some online journals compensate for these limitations by using standard principles of transliteration to represent words in non-Roman fonts, surrounding underlines to indicate an italicized word or title (*e.g.*, _Computing in Musicology_), surrounding asterisks to indicate boldface (*e.g.*, ASCII 130 should *not* be used in online texts to represent é), and other similar methods. It would, of course, also be possible to include these more complex elements by imposing certain limitations on the programs and machines that might be used to view or search them and by transmitting the texts over the networks in encoded form, but this would be contrary to the *TML*'s aim of providing the most universal access.

Although the 95 characters and a few control codes are limiting, it is still possible to produce and transmit texts of some complexity. Because of the nature of the texts and their anticipated use, the *TML* was less concerned with matters of typography than with indicating various text-critical matters, page breaks, editorial insertions, and especially the musical notation and graphic material that abounds in medieval Latin music theory. Two documents, the "Principles of Orthography" and the "Table of Codes for Noteshapes and Rests," were accordingly developed. They define simple and largely mnemonic uses of available symbols to indicate necessary parts of the text *and* make it possible for these parts to be intelligently searched. These documents are reproduced as Appendices 1 and 2 at the end of this article.

Data Capture and Verification

No database can, of course, be any better than the quality of its data. Although this is not strictly a technical matter pertaining to character sets, it is important to note that any text file must be carefully prepared, checked against its source, and reviewed to insure that there are no extraneous codes or inadvertent characters. In the *TML*, data entry is first accomplished by a combination of optical character recognition (OCR) and manual keying.[10] Texts from manuscripts or incunabula that exhibit highly irregular fonts and numerous typographic abbreviations are keyed by hand. Texts from more modern editions, such as the Coussemaker *Scriptores*, can be scanned and corrected. The precise mix of manual keying and scanning and the configuration of hardware and software differs at each of the TML Centers, but it may be generalized as follows: scanning is done on an Apple Scanner or a similar sort of machine, reading into a Macintosh IIci or comparable CPU with 8 or more megabytes of RAM; the scan is then read by a program for OCR, such as ExperVision's *TypeReader* or Caere's *OmniPage*. The ASCII file produced by the scanner is edited for content and corrected. All material—whether scanned or keyed, previously published or manuscript—is then compared at least twice with the original source before being placed in the database: the first review is typically done by the member of the TML Project Committee supervising the graduate assistants working at the local TML Center or by a member of the Editorial Advisory Committee. The file is then sent to the Indiana University TML Center, where it is checked once again and the necessary corrections are entered. After these final corrections are entered, the data file is locked, reviewed by the Project Director, and prepared for entry into the database.

---

[10] Although the TML Project Committee initially had some reservation about the reliability and cost-efficiency of OCR, three years' trial with the system and a comparison of the two methods has shown it to be somewhat faster, more accurate, and consequently less expensive than manual inputting of modern printed material. This is due in part to the unique nature of Latin music treatises, which are often highly formulaic and repetitive and which usually incorporate a considerable amount of musical notation and graphic material. When material is keyed by hand, the same sorts of errors well known to students of scribal technique are encountered. First, the formulaic nature of the text makes it extremely easy for the human eye to skip from one phrase to its parallel and omit substantial quantities of text. This type of error cannot be made by a scanner and program for OCR. Second, the repetitive character of the text makes it extremely

Text Files: Delivery and Structure

The *TML* delivers its data to subscribers through either of two parallel systems: the *TML-L*, which is operated by LISTSERV; or the *TML-FTP*, which provides normal FTP access.[11] A variety of factors (the address of the subscriber's return path, the definitions of the preferences for delivery at each of the Bitnet nodes, the number of intervening gateways, the configuration of a subscriber's mail utility, etc.) affect the manner in which the data is delivered, but it will most commonly arrive as a Bitnet file, as mail, or as the result of an FTP transfer. Unless the data files are to be stored in alternative forms, each one suitable to a particular mode of delivery, it is necessary to structure the files so that they can survive the most restrictive—but still quite common—mode of delivery: *i.e.*, electronic mail with an 80-character limit per line.

After the data in each *TML* file has been checked several times and all the necessary corrections have been made, it is then prepared for entry into the *TML-L* and *TML-FTP* (electronic archives). To enable it to survive transfer through various mailers (and therefore to be moved to an individual mainframe account upon arrival and then displayed and searched on the mainframe or downloaded to a personal computer), there must be no ASCII character beyond the basic set, no line of the file may have more than 80 characters, each line must end with a "return" (ASCII 13 or its equivalent as the file is translated from system to system), and all returns must be followed by a linefeed (ASCII 10 or its equivalent). First, every file is searched for characters beyond the basic set. Then, in order to distinguish between returns marking the ends of paragraphs and those marking the ends of lines, each paragraph is terminated by a double return; blank lines in the text intended to set off a heading (for example) are expanded to double blank lines. The entire file is then converted into a 9-point monospaced font, with one-inch

---

tedious, and in consequence, the number of errors made in manual keying increases dramatically as the day wears on. By contrast, a number of different activities are involved in OCR, and they can be grouped for efficiency and to provide the variety that helps keep the mind alert (for example, at the Indiana University TML Center, we typically begin by photocopying an entire treatise with some enlargement and darkening, then we scan all the pages, then each scan is subjected to OCR and added to the data file, and the complete data file is then corrected). In addition, it must be noted that basic clerical data entry is not of much use with this material: suspensions and abbreviations need to be expanded (which requires that the assistant must be able to read Latin, at least at a basic level), flags for graphic material must be entered, and notation must be encoded (which requires that the assistant be able to read it).

[11] These systems and their relationship to the *TML* were discussed in last year's issue of *CM* (see n. 5 *supra*).

margins on the left and right; this results in a line of exactly 80 characters. To insure that no lines are broken at improper or confusing places (for example, between the hyphen and the number in a page flag or in the middle of a long string of encoded notation), the entire file is reviewed line-by-line and a string improperly broken at the end of a line is forced onto the next line. Then the file is saved as a text-only file with line breaks; the line breaks (*i.e.*, returns) are subsequently converted into line breaks followed by linefeeds.

After the data files of the *TML* have been transferred to a local system, they are ready to be read and searched. Although most mainframes do have some sort of searching capabilities within their text viewers or editors and these may be suitable for certain users, the *TML* assumes that most users will want to download the files to their personal computers in order to take advantage of a search engine such as *GOfer* or *WordCruncher*.

The *TML* Introduction provides detailed instructions on downloading, excerpts of which follow:

> Every mainframe will have a different selection of error-correction protocols available, but most should have at least *Kermit* and *Xmodem*. Each communications program and modem addresses these protocols in different ways, and this Introduction cannot substitute for your instruction manuals. There are, however, a few points to keep in mind when you download files from your mainframe.

> Subscribers with IBM or DOS computers:

> You will not need to do anything special when you download the files or when you search them using the recommended search program, *GOfer*. . . . They have been configured with the necessary carriage returns and line feeds to display properly on any DOS machine (you may, however, have to adjust the font size and margins to fit your monitor or printer). Set your communications program so that it does NOT filter out any characters.

> Subscribers with Macintosh computers:

> If you are planning to use the *TML* simply to display texts to read on your screen or to search for single words, you need only filter out the line feeds (ASCII 10) that will appear at the beginning of each line of text. Some communications programs (such as *White Knight*) allow you to do this in the course of downloading, but it can also be done simply by using the "search and replace" utility that exists in most word processors (the manual for your word processor should tell you how to enter an ASCII code in the utility).

If you would like to convert the files to pure Macintosh files (*i.e.*, with a carriage return [ASCII 13] only at the ends of full paragraphs), you can do this in the following fashion:

1. Remove all the line feeds at the beginning of each line (if not already done).

2. Using your word processor's "search and replace" utility, instruct it to find all double carriage returns (in Microsoft *Word*, for example, you would enter [without quotation marks] "^13^13" in the "Find What:" box) and change them to ASCII 30 (in Microsoft *Word*, you would enter [without quotation marks] "^30" in the "Change To:" box). Sometimes the process of downloading a file will add a space between the double carriage returns, and if your change utility does not find any ^13^13 patterns, this has probably occurred. In this case, repeat the process but add a space to the two ASCII codes (in Microsoft *Word*, enter [without quotation marks] "^13^32^13" in the "Find What:" box).

3. Using your word processor's "search and replace" utility once again, instruct it to find all single carriage returns (in Microsoft *Word*, you would enter [without quotation marks] "^13" in the "Find What:" box) and change them to a space (in Microsoft *Word*, you would enter [without quotation marks] "^32" in the "Change To:" box).

4. Finally, use your word processor's "search and replace" utility to find ASCII 30 (in Microsoft *Word*, you would enter [without quotation marks] "^30" in the "Find What:" box) and change it to a single carriage return (in Microsoft *Word*, you would enter [without quotation marks] "^13" in the "Change To:" box).

If you use *White Knight* as your communications program, all this can be done automatically by selecting "Paragraph format" under the "File transfer" option of the "Customize" menu. Other communications programs may also be able to do this; please consult your manual.

Graphics Files

Latin music theory regularly includes abundant figures and musical notation for which no ASCII equivalents exist. This material cannot simply be omitted. Musical notation that can be precisely entered as codes (see Appendix 2) has been encoded in the ASCII text file, while full musical examples or figures are scanned, saved in GIF format, and flagged to locations within the text files themselves.[12] If the example includes text, this is given in the ASCII file within brackets (see the example in Appendix 1).[13] It is important to note that the codes and flags enable most of the graphic material to be subject to the same sort of intelligent searching provided for the text itself.

When the user looks for a word or text string, the search engine locates and displays this material within the graphics flags as well as within the treatise proper. Likewise, by employing the proper code for a notational symbol, the user can instruct the search engine to locate every occurrence of a noteshape. By combining codes with words or text strings in the search, the user can simultaneously discover graphic, notational, and textual references within the data set. Thus, users with graphics capabilities on their machines are able to both search and display text as well as musical notation and figures. Although users without graphics capabilities cannot display graphics, they are still able to search all parts of the database.

Graphics files, by their nature, are more complex than the text files. To insure that they are not corrupted in the course of being transferred over the various networks, they are first UUencoded. Once decoded, they may be displayed directly in the Macintosh environment by using any program that interprets GIF files; MS-DOS computers must be properly configured to display graphics, and if so configured, the GIF file may either be displayed directly or readily translated into a compatible format. Although standardization is currently lacking in graphics formats, the GIF format is the most generally accessible, and graphics formats are continually becoming more compatible.[14]

Closing Comment

Because the *TML* is composed of ASCII text and GIF graphics, it can be used by any machine with its own search program. This structure also makes it possible to adapt the files to other systems of delivery that may become feasible or popular in the coming decades. While by no means the only method for handling a full-text database, the *TML* does have the advantage of making its data available with a minimum of limitations for the user.

---

[12] The GIF format was selected over any other format for several reasons: GIF files are quite small, and the format can be read on mainframes and on any of the major hardware configurations with simple GIF viewers available as free- or shareware.

[13] The text, of course, also appears in the graphics file that stores the figure, table, or musical example itself.

[14] UUencoding (see n. 7 *supra*) was selected over other encoding systems because of its general availability across systems as diverse as Macintosh, MS-DOS, and mainframes. Full instructions for retrieving, decoding, and displaying graphics files are provided by the *TML*, and free- or shareware UUdecoders and GIF viewers are made available by the *TML* to its subscribers.

Appendix 1. **Principles of Orthography for the *TML*.**

1. Text

Text data files produced from printed or manuscript sources will retain as exactly as possible the original spelling, punctuation, and capitalization, with the following exceptions:

1. In manuscript sources (but not in printed material) **i/j**, **u/v**, **c/t** before i plus vowel will be normalized.
2. In printed material, **small caps** will be converted to upper- or lower-case letters as the context requires (Roman numerals will always be entered as upper-case letters).
3. In printed material, *corrigenda* published as a part of the book itself should be entered (but see ¶1e below).
4. **Accented letters** will be entered without accents.
5. **Suspensions** and **abbreviations** will be expanded.[1]
6. **Periods, commas, colons**, or *paragraphi* will always be placed on the baseline.
7. **Proper nouns** will be capitalized.
8. **Initial letters** of titles and true *incipits* will be capitalized, but initial letters of obvious or apparent fragments will not be capitalized.
9. **Non-roman letters**, which are not part of the standard ASCII character set, will be entered as capitalized letter-names between brackets (*e.g.*, Γ will be entered as [Gamma]); words written in non-roman letters will be transliterated according to the standards of the *Chicago Manual of Style*, 13th edition.
10. In order to preserve the lining of poetry, a hard return (ASCII code 13) will be entered at the **end of** each **line**.
11. **Double letters** set one above the other (*e.g.*, $\overset{e}{e}$) will be entered side by side (*e.g.*, ee).

Various types of symbols are available and will be used in data files that will be stored as ASCII files readable on any machine.[2]

1. Single brackets ([= ASCII code 91;] = ASCII code 93) will enclose the following six types of material:
    a. **Codes showing the beginning of each page** or folio side, surrounded by hyphens. For example, [-2-] will indicate the beginning of page 2 in text drawn from a published (or paginated) work; [-f.22v-] will indicate the beginning of the verso of folio 22 in text drawn from a manuscript (or foliated) work.
    b. **Codes for musical notation** appearing within a sentence (see Table of Codes and the section on musical notation below).

---

[1] Abbreviated cardinal or ordinal numbers (*e.g.*, 2ª, 4ª, 3ᵘˢ, etc.) should be expanded when the result can be expressed as a single word (*e.g.*, secunda, quarta, tritus, etc.) but otherwise should be left in abbreviated form (*e.g.*, 1340o). Roman and Arabic numerals should be left as numerals.

[2] *i.e.*, alphanumeric codes 32-126.

  c. **Editorial notes** indicating the presence of **figures, tables,** or a **musical example**. For each example, a separate line will exhibit a reference to the source (*e.g.*, [Berkeley p. 88] or [Madrid, Biblioteca Nacional, 6486, f. 22v]).

  If the example is **accompanied by text**, this will be included within the brackets (*e.g.*, [Berkeley p. 86; text: E-la, D-la-sol, C-sol-fa, B-fa-B-mi, A-la-mi-re, G-sol-re-ut, F-fa-ut, E-la-mi, D-la-sol-re, C-sol-fa-ut, D-sol-re, C-fa-ut, B-mi, A-re, Gamma-ut, 5 superacute, 7 acute, 8 graves, Declaracio manus secundum usum]) to enable the search program to locate and display text strings within figures as well as within the text proper. The text, of course, will also appear in the graphics file that will store the figure, table, or musical example itself.[3]

  d. **Text added by later hands**[4] (noted following the text: m.sec. or m.alt. or m.rec.), especially marginal hands (noted following the text: in marg.).

  e. **Corrections added to the base text**, either above the line (noted: corr. supra lin.) or in the margin (noted: corr. in marg.).

  f. **Non-Roman letter-names**.

2. Double brackets ([[   ]]) will enclose **letters or words cancelled** in the manuscript itself.

3. Angle brackets (< = ASCII code 60; > = ASCII code 62) will enclose

  a. letters, words, or **passages read by conjecture**; or

  b. if a short passage cannot be certainly transcribed, dots indicating the approximate number of letters.

In the very few cases where an entire passage may be illegible, the number of lines followed by "legi non potest" will be noted within the angle brackets.

4. Braces ({ = ASCII code 123; } = ASCII code 125) will surround an **interpolated passage** to show the approximate transposition.

5. The asterisk (* = ASCII code 42) will be used as equivalent to the **obelus** (†).

2. Musical notation

All musical symbols or notation that appear within sentences of the text will be entered as codes. In general, single-line examples—especially examples with no specific pitch content—should also be encoded. See the *Table of Codes for Noteshapes and Rests*. Polyphonic or more complex musical examples, charts, figures, graphs, and similar sorts of material that cannot be keyed as ASCII text (which may, of course, include the use of spaces to lay out simple tables) will be scanned, saved in GIF format, and keyed to the original location in the printed or manuscript source.

---

[3] The figures themselves will be stored and retrievable as GIF files.

[4] Including glosses and scholia.

Appendix 2.
Table of Codes for Noteshapes, Rests, Ligatures, Mensuration Signs, Clefs, and Miscellaneous Figures.

Noteshape codes are placed between brackets and must appear in the order given in this table. Each group of symbols under N, P, L, or M appears together with no spaces or punctuation; each noteshape, rest, ligature, mensuration sign, clef, or miscellaneous figure is separated from the following one by a comma.

Noteshapes

N1. Multiples[1]	
Quadruplex	4
Triplex	3
Duplex	2

N2. Shapes		
Maxima		MX
Longa		L
Brevis		B
Semibrevis		S
Minima		M
Semiminima		SM
Addita		A
Fusa		F

N3. Coloration	
nigra[2]	b
vacua	v
rubea	r
semivacua	sv
semirubea	sr

N4. Tails[3]	
cauda	c
plica	p
cauda yrundinis	cy

N5. Direction[4]	
sursum	s
deorsum	d
dextre	dx
sinistre	sn
oblique	o

---

[1] Optional. May only be applied to the *maxima* and *longa*.

[2] The symbol "b" is to be used only in ligatures exhibiting more than one color as specified in n. 9 *infra*. In all other cases, black is the color assumed unless otherwise noted.

[3] Indicated only if the tail varies from the basic shape pictured in N2.

[4] Always indicated in ligature codes; otherwise, only if direction differs from the basic shape pictured in N2.

N6. Flags[5]	
vexilla [preceded by number[6]]	**vx**
retorta	**vxrt**
dextre	**vxdx**
sinistre	**vxsn**

Rests

P1. Multiples (optional)	
Quadruplex	**4**
Triplex	**3**
Duplex	**2**

P2. Shapes	
Maxima	**MXP**
Longa	**LP**[7]
Brevis	**BP**
Semibrevis	**SP**
Minima	**MP**
Semiminima	**SMP**
Addita	**AP**
Fusa	**FP**

Ligatures[8]

L1. Ligatures are indicated by "Lig" followed (in this order and as applicable) by:

    (1) the number of notes in the ligature;

    (2) coloration (see N3 above);[9]

    (3) cs or cd and the side on which the tail appears (see N4-5 above); and

    (4) the intervals in order, with "a" for ascending and "d" for descending, with additional tails indicated in the order in which they appear.[10]

If a subsequent note in a ligature is turned back over the preceding note (as in the *podatus*, *porrectus*, liquescent neumes, plicas, etc.), the letter indicating the interval is followed by "rt." For example:

would equal [M,M,M,M,S,B,pt, Lig2cssnod,Lig4cssnaodacddx, pt,Lig5aadd,MX].

---

[5] Flags are assumed to be drawn on the oblique to the right side of the tail, unless otherwise indicated. In this section, *dx* and *sn* mean that the flag appears at a right angle to the tail and points left or right.

[6] Indicated by numeral only if greater than one.

[7] If the context calls for differentiating between perfect and imperfect *longa* rests, this may be done by using 2LP and 3LP.

---

[8] All notes are assumed to be square, unless the reference to the interval is preceded by "o" (for oblique) or "cu" (for *conjuncturae* or *currentes*).

[9] If the ligature exhibits more than one color, "r," "v," or "b" precede the codes of (3) and (4) to indicate the point at which the color changes.

[10] Except in the case of a *longa* or a *maxima* **within** a ligature (this exception does not apply to the **final** note of the ligature), which is indicated as "L" or "MX" following the interval that precedes it or following the codes of (1), (2), and (3) if it is the first note of the ligature. In ligatures, MX is assumed to refer only to the extended rectangular notehead; if it also has a tail, the location and direction are indicated. Note the example under "Barlines or multiple examples on a single staff."

Mensuration and Proportion Signs

M1. Shape	
Circle	**O**
Semicircle open on the right	**C**
Semicircle open on the left	**CL**
Semicircle open on the top	**CT**
Semicircle open on the bottom	**CB**
Rectangle	**R**
Triangle	**TR**

M2. Internal marks	
dot (preceded by a number if more than one)	**d**
descending vertical line (preceded by a number if more than one)	**rvd**
ascending vertical line (preceded by a number if more than one)	**rvs**
horizontal line extending right (preceded by a number if more than one)	**rhdx**
horizontal line extending left (preceded by a number if more than one)	**rhsn**

M3. Proportions

The presence of the line of *diminutio* is indicated by "dim" following the symbols of M1 and M2. Fractional proportions are simply indicated by the two numbers separated by a virgule (*e.g.*, 3/2).

Clefs

If the clef is shown on a staff, a number is appended indicating the line on which the clef appears (counting from the bottom of the staff), with two numbers separated by a hyphen indicating that the clef appears in the space between the two lines (for example, ClefG2 or ClefC3-4).

C clef	**ClefC**
F clef	**ClefF**
G clef	**ClefG**

Miscellaneous

square b	**sqb**
round b	**rob**
punctus (of whatever type)	**pt**
a small line extending above and below a staff line **not** functioning as one of the rests	**r**

double letters set one above the other (*e.g.* $\overset{e}{e}$) are entered side by side (*e.g.*, ee).

A vacant staff is indicated by "staff," followed by a number indicating the number of lines in the staff (*e.g.*, staff4 or staff5); "on staff" following a set of notation codes indicates that all the preceding notation appeared on a staff. If additional codes follow, this indicates that the staff ended while the notation continued.

Barlines or multiple examples on a single staff

If several illustrative passages appear in a single example, a semicolon (;) followed by a space indicates the presence of a single or double bar separating one passage from another. If a single passage includes barlines, these may also be indicated by a semicolon followed by a space. Here is an example of such a case:

This would be encoded as [ClefF3, Lig2MXcddxaMXcddx; Lig2MXdMX, Lig2MXaMXcddx on staff4].

Appendix 3. Associated TML Centers.

1. Louisiana State University: Jan Herlinger, School of Music, Louisiana State University, Baton Rouge, LA 70803; fax: (504) 388-2568; e-mail: *MUJNH@LSUVM.BITNET*.

2. Ohio State University: Charles M. Atkinson, School of Music, 1899 College Road, Columbus, OH 43210; fax: (614) 292-1102; e-mail: *cmatkins@magnus.acs.ohio-state.edu*.

3. Princeton University: Thomas Walker, Department of Music, Woolworth Music Center, Princeton University, Princeton, NJ 08544; e-mail: *trwalker@pucc.bitnet*.

4. University of Colorado at Boulder: Oliver B. Ellsworth. College of Music, University of Colorado, Campus Box 301, Boulder, CO 80309; e-mail: *Ellsworth_O@cubldr.colorado.edu*.

5. University of Nebraska: Peter M. Lefferts, School of Music, University of Nebraska, 120 Westbrook Music Building, Lincoln, NE 68588-0100; tel.: (402) 472-2507; e-mail: *lefferts @unlinfo.unl.edu*.

Reference

A printed guide, the *TML: Canon of Data Files*, which is published annually, contains a general introduction and bibliographic records for all files. The current (4th) edition (Bloomington: TML, 1993) is available free of charge by writing to the Center.

Further information: Thomas J. Mathiesen, Project Director, Thesaurus Musicarum Latinarum, Department of Musicology, School of Music, Indiana University, Bloomington, IN 47405; tel.: (812) 855-5471 or 876-3592; e-mail: *Mathiese@INDIANA.BITNET* or *Mathiese@Ucs.Indiana.Edu*.

Ruth Steiner

CANTUS

CANTUS is a database of indices of the chants of the Divine Office contained in manuscript and early printed sources. Its holdings are now available via Gopher on the Internet. Select from the menus presented (1) other Gopher servers, (2) North America, (3) USA, (4) Washington, D.C., (5) The Catholic University of America, and (6) Special Resources. Then read the file *ABOUT_CANTUS*.

In the Divine Office sacred texts were presented before large congregations as lessons and chants that were repeated yearly. The texts, which were derived from Biblical commentaries and biographies of saints, were often adapted to local or special needs. In comparison with texts that were merely spoken, sung texts were better memorized and probably had greater cultural impact. The influence of the Divine Office was strong in the Middle Ages, when chants borrowed from it were often included in dramas.

The database dramatically improves access to primary sources of the Divine Office. Each chant in a source is listed as one record. Concise, self-explanatory abbreviations for genre and liturgical function are included in the record, as are the sigla for important sources in which the chant appears. Records can therefore be easily sorted and selected from a file. The total number of records is approaching 50,000.

Complete indices are currently available for the following sources:

- Bamberg, Staatsbibliothek, lit. 25
- Karlsruhe, Badische Landesbibliothek, Aug. LX
- Toledo, Biblioteca Capitular, 44.1 and 44.2
- Piacenza, Biblioteca Capitolare, 65
- Florence, Biblioteca Laurenziana, Conv. Sopp. 560
- Florence, Arcivescovado, s.c.
- Paris, Bibliothèque Nationale, n. a. lat. 1535
- Cambrai, Bibliothèque Municipale, 38 and XVIC4

There is also an index for the antiphons of the Sarum antiphoner. An index for one source may be used separately or jointly with other indices. The preparation of additional indices is expected to continue for several years. *CANTUS* files have also provided the foundation for a series of bibliographical publications offered by the Institute of Mediaeval Music in Ottawa.

Files may be requested by Internet from the project director or retrieved using Gopher. Diskettes are also available with a small charge to cover the costs of processing and mailing. Indices are sent as ASCII files. They can be used with *dBase* and other database programs and also with word processing programs such as *Word-Perfect*. Users are also invited to use material in existing indices to speed the preparation of indices of additional sources.

Further information: Ruth Steiner, Project Director, CANTUS, The Benjamin T. Rome School of Music, The Catholic University of America, Washington, DC 20064; tel.: (202) 319-5415; fax: 319-6280; e-mail: *steiner@cua.edu*.   The Institute of Mediaeval Music is located at 1270 Lampman Crescent, Ottawa, Ontario, Canada K2C 1P8.

Mark Whitney

The Chanson, 1400-1600:
A Multiple-Access Catalogue

The Chanson, 1400-1600 is a comprehensive index of bibliographic information pertaining to the fifteenth- and sixteenth-century chanson.   The index comprises several thousand entries arranged alphabetically by textual incipit. Included are all items in Daschner (1962), with updated RISM-style source listings and concordances, and the French secular works preserved in the manuscripts described in the University of Illinois Census-Catalogue (1979-1988).   Included also are incipits for all identifiable monophonic chansons of the period, chansons cited in secular plays, chanson-derived instrumental compositions, noëls, chansons quoted in *fricassées*, and incipits of poetic texts which appear to have been associated with music at one time, even though the associated music may no longer be extant (as is true, for example, of several of the texts in Jeffery 1971, 1976). The index also identifies all cases in which one chanson is derived from another.

Each first-level entry provides a textual incipit, author of the text (where known), nonmusical sources of the text, and all known musical settings of the text.   The second-level entry for each musical setting is accompanied by a complete list of sources, facsimiles, modern editions, and recordings.

The final version will be made available in three formats: (1) hard copy, indexed by source, composer, poet, publisher, etc.; (2) word processing files, formatted for widely used applications such as *WordPerfect*, *Word*, and *Nota Bene*; and (3) ASCII files, delimited for downloading to relational databases such as Microsoft *Access* and Alpha *Four*.

The database versions will generate annotated lists, or "reports," of selected information, *e.g.*, works of a given composer or group of composers, works in a given source or group of sources, all works based on a given model, settings of the works of a given poet, works issued by a given publisher, and so forth.

References

Daschner, Hubert. "Die Gedruckten mehrstimmigen Chansons von 1500-1600: Literarische Quellen und Bibliographie." Inaugural Dissertation, Rheinischen Friedrich-Wilhelms-Universität, Bonn, 1962.

Jeffery, Brian, ed. *Chanson Verse of the Early Renaissance*. London: Tecla Editions, 1971, 1976.

University of Illinois, Renaissance Archives for Manuscript Studies. *Census-Catalogue of Manuscript Sources of Polyphonic Music, 1400-1550*. American Institute of Musicology, 1979-88.

Further information: Mark Whitney, 3311 Morrow Ave., Waco, TX 76707; tel.: (817) 752-2169.

Patricia Elliott

Beethoven Bibliography Online

The *Beethoven Bibliography Database*

The *Beethoven Bibliography Database* is a special database in the online catalog of the San Jose (California) State University Library. It uses the *Innopac* software developed by Innovative Interfaces of Berkeley, California. Cataloging records for the Beethoven Center's collection are tape-loaded from the Online Computer Library Center (OCLC); other records are encoded in Machine Readable Cataloging (MARC) format and keyed directly into the database through dedicated terminals. The project is directed by William Meredith and Patricia Elliott.

Access and dissemination

The Beethoven Bibliography Database is available through the Internet via telnet.

Telnet address:	**SJSULIB.SJSU.EDU**
Login:	**LIB**
Choose option D:	**d > CONNECT to another database**

This choice will lead to a second screen with the option of connecting to the Beethoven Bibliography Database. Further instructions are given on the screen.

Contents

The goal of the *Bibliography Database* is to provide researchers with a tool to improve access to information about Beethoven's life and music. The bibliography includes significant literature on Beethoven of varying types and formats (monographs, serials, essays in books, journal articles, dissertations, etc.); listings of scores of Beethoven's works; and manuscript sources. Research materials published in all languages and writings from fields outside of music are cited. Information on locations of primary sources in collections all over the world will eventually be included.

The database allows for combined searches by names, titles, main and minor subjects, genres, opus numbers, library locations, publishers, languages, and dates, among other options. The database currently consists of 2,700 bibliographic records and will grow to an estimated 22,000 works by the year 2004. The Beethoven Center intends to update the bibliography on an ongoing basis.

The *Beethoven Thesaurus*

The auxiliary *Beethoven Thesaurus*, a list of subject indexing terms used for the project, is maintained using the Liu-Palmer Thesaurus Construction System, which runs on an IBM-AT compatible computer. Printed copies of the *Beethoven Thesaurus* are available through subscription. For information on access, contact Patricia Elliott at the address below.

Further information: Patricia Elliott, Center for Beethoven Studies, San Jose State University, One Washington Square, San Jose, CA 95192-0171; tel. (408) 924-4590; fax: 924-4365; e-mail: *elliott@sjsuvm1.sjsu.edu*.

Kimberly C. Walls
The Music Research Information Service

MRIS, the Music Research Information Service, is an electronic gateway to information about resources related to music education, psychology, therapy, and medicine. It is based at the Institute for Music Research at the University of Texas at San Antonio and is sponsored by a strategic initiative grant from the university. *MRIS* also provides access to the *CAIRSS* (music research literature) and *TIME* (software archives) databases explained below.

MRIS contains calls for papers, conference announcements, research news, product announcements, and appeals for research assistance. *MRIS*, *CAIRSS*, and *TIME* are being updated continually. The *MRIS* and *TIME* projects are directed by Kimberly C. Walls. The *CAIRSS* database is maintained by Don Hodges.

Access

MRIS, *CAIRSS*, and *TIME* may be searched free of charge by persons with access to telnet or Gopher via the Internet.

Telnet address:	*runner.utsa.edu*
Login:	**imr**
Password:	**< return >**

All other instructions, including Gopher commands, are on the screen. The option "other music services" produces an extensive list of online resources for music research.

Alternatively *MRIS* may be reached by Gopher (*runner.utsa.edu 3000*) or directly by modem (2400 baud or greater) at (210) 561-8000. At the "Local >" prompt type **c** *runner*. Then follow the telnet instructions.

CAIRSS and TIME

The *CAIRSS* (Computer-Assisted Information Retrieval Service System) database is a NOTIS database of music research articles from over 1,000 journals. Articles may be searched using keywords such as subject and author. *CAIRSS* was initiated in November 1992.

TIME (Technology in Music Education) is a comprehensive database of music software which will be available beginning in Fall 1993. *TIME* includes publisher's descriptions, independent reviews, and availability information for all types of music software which may be useful to music educators. In addition to the software database, IMR will serve as a repository of music introduction software which may be viewed by potential users.

Contributions

Contributions of software lists, software reviews, and software to be published in *TIME* are being solicited. Contributions from musicians who are familiar with a product, from publishers, and from developers are welcome. All contributions are properly credited in the database. Software products which might be useful in teaching/learning about music or related subjects are eligible for the database. Computer software and software products such as instructional videotapes, videodiscs, CD-ROMs, and classroom systems will be included.

Contributors may send listings of products and publisher's descriptions either as a hard copy, on 3 1/2" diskette (Mac or MS-DOS), or e-mail to the project coordinator. Product information or review should include as many as possible of the following items:

(1) Product name/title
(2) Publication date
(3) Version number
(4) Publisher name
(5) Author/programmer's name(s)
(6) Hardware requirements such as type of computer, MIDI,
peripherals, etc.
(7) Publisher's description
(8) Availability (names, addresses, phone numbers of distributors,
price of product, educational discounts, etc.)

Further information-*MRIS* and *TIME*: Kimberly C. Walls, Institute for Music Research, 6900 North Loop 1604 West, San Antonio, TX 78249; tel.: (210) 691-5321, e-mail: *kwalls@lonestar. utsa.edu*.

Further information-*CAIRSS*: Don Hodges, Director, Institute for Music Research, University of Texas at San Antonio, 6900 North Loop 1604 West, San Antonio, TX 78249-0645; tel.: (210) 691-5317; e-mail: *dhodges@lonestar.utsa.edu*.

Lee Rothfarb

Music Theory Online

Music Theory Online, a publication of the Society for Music Theory (ISSN 1067-3040) is an electronic journal for music theory. It contains articles, reviews, dissertation listings, announcements, and job listings. Established provisionally at the Fall 1992 meeting of the Society, *MTO* is now being published on a continuing basis.

Access
Those interested in subscribing to *MTO* may send an e-mail message to one of the following two addresses:

listserv@husc.harvard.edu   [Internet]
listserv@husc.bitnet   [Bitnet]

Leave the "Subject:" line blank.

As the text of the message include the single line:

subscribe mto-list < YourFirstName YourLastName >

[Please note that *mto-list* is a recent change from *mto-j* and should be substituted in all commands in which the list name is used.]

A welcome message will arrive once the subscription request has been processed. This message explains how to retrieve *MTO* documentation. It includes the table of contents for the current issue, which explains how to retrieve *MTO* items. Subscribers may retrieve an index (*mto.index*) from *mto-serv* using the **get** command.

Questions to the moderator may be addressed to:

mto-editor@husc.harvard.edu   [Internet]
mto-editor@husc.bitnet   [Bitnet]

MTO documentation gives information on retrieving single items and item types (*e.g.*, job listings), guidelines for authors and editorial policy, and instructions for online searches of the *MTO* database. The document types are

> *art* = article
> *gif* = musical example(s)
> *rev* = review
> *tlk* = commentary
> *dis* = dissertation listings
> *ann* = announcements
> *job* = job listings
> *toc* = table of contents

To get a current list of all files in the *MTO* archive, request the document called *mto.index* from *mto-serv*.

In order to retrieve items from past issues, subscribers must specify the desired item(s) by standardized *MTO* filenames (as they appear in an *MTO* table of contents). Filenames will be in the following form: *mto.yy.v.i.author.xxx*, where yy = year, v = vol. no., i = issue no., *author* = author's name, and xxx = the item-type [as above]. Replace yy with the last two digits of the year, v with the volume number, i with the issue number, etc., as in *mto.93.0.1.neumeyer.art*.

Retrieving Material

MTO shares many elements of its basic method of document preparation and distribution with the *TML* [see pp. 33-48]. The musical examples and graphical figures for *MTO* are provided in the Graphical Interchange Format, GIF for short (pronounced JIF). Like all graphical files, GIFs are made up of binary code and cannot be safely mailed over telecommunications networks.

In order to be e-mailed without danger of corruption, the GIFs must be encoded, "UUencoded" to be precise (UU = Unix-to-Unix, referring [originally] to the transfer of files from one Unix machine to another). The UUencoding converts the binary GIFs into plain ASCII text, which is safe for e-mailing. Once received, the UUencoded GIFs must be UUdecoded (converted back to binary form), before they can be viewed. GIF files, like all graphical files, tend to be quite large. Beware of requesting many GIFs at once! The examples will arrive, UUencoded, in e-mail messages. Save the messages as files and download them to your desktop machine. Once the files are on your desktop machine, decode them using the decoding software supplied by *MTO* (instructions included with the software). Finally, view them with the GIF viewing software provided by *MTO*.

MTO provides software for UUdecoding and for viewing musical examples on both IBM and Macintosh computers. Retrieve the document named *software.txt* for more information.

If your mainframe is connected to the Internet, you can retrieve examples (and other filetypes) with FTP (File Transfer Protocol), and avoid the coding/decoding processes. Implementations of FTP differ, so universally valid instructions are not possible. Consult your local user services for assistance. The general procedure is as follows:

At mainframe prompt:	**ftp** *husc4.harvard.edu*
Login:	**anonymous**
Password:	**guest**
At **ftp>** prompt:	**cd** *pub/smt/mto* [changes to *MTO* directory]
At **ftp>** prompt:	**binary** [prepares FTP for a binary transfer]
At **ftp>** prompt:	**get** *FileName.gif* [retrieves an example file]

Repeat the "get" command for all desired GIFs, or other filetypes (*.art*, *.rev*, etc.). Transfer files retrieved to your mainframe to your personal computer.

Contributions

Send all announcements (about regional and national conferences, workshops, lectures, lecture series, awards and grants, etc.) to the General Editor. There is no special format for announcements, but the text should include all important information, *e.g.*, time, place, fees, deadline, contacts. Templates are available for submission of information on new dissertations and job listings.

Further information: Lee Rothfarb, *MTO* General Editor, is on leave in 1993-4, but he may be reached electronically at the editorial addresses given above. From August 1994 he will be at the Department of Music, University of California at Santa Barbara, Santa Barbara, CA 93106.

Other Electronic Resources

Supplementing our article "Using Networks in Musical Research" (*Computing in Musicology*, Vol. 8, pp. 33-54), we append additional information about moderated discussions in Table 1 (see p. 58). These range from two discussions maintained by the music programs in individual institutions (the City University of New York Graduate Center and the University of Utah School of Music) through four lists concerned with specific repertories (one for the Middle Ages and Renaissance, one for the lute, opera in general, operetta) to two lists serving collectors (of 78 r.p.m. records) and restorers (of pipe organs).

Many additional network discussions for music exist. An extensive compilation of these is maintained by Kara Robinson at Kent State University in Ohio. She may be contacted as *krobinso@kentvm.kent.edu*.

Moderators of additional network discussion and electronic conferences related to music are invited to send word of their services to CCARH, 525 Middlefield Road, Ste. 120, Menlo Park, CA 94025; e-mail: *XB.L36@forsythe.stanford.edu*.

List Name	Subject	Moderator	Access type	Subscription address
CUNY Graduate Center	Graduate level music scholarship discussion	Bob Kosovsky, Theresa Muir	listserver	*LISTSERV@CUNYVMS1. GC.CUNY.EDU*
LUTE	Lute music and performance	Wayne Cripps	Internet conference	*LUTE-INFO@ CS.DARTMOUTH.EDU*
MED-AND-REN-MUSIC	Practical and research queries related to medieval and Renaissance music	Isobel Preece	Internet conference	*med-and-ren-music-request@mailbase.ac.uk*
OPERA-L	Opera research	F. A. de M. A. Doria	listserver	*MAILSERV@BRFAPQ. BITNET*; also *MAILSERV%BRFAPQ. BITNET@ VM1.NODAK.EDU*
PIPEORG-L	Pipe organs: technical and historical data	Dave Schutt, Ben Chi	listserver	*LISTSERV@ALBANY. EDU*
SAVOYNET	Gilbert and Sullivan; operetta	Ralph MacPhail, Jr.; Wm. C. Venman	Internet conference	*SAVOYNET-REQUEST@CESSC. BRIDGEWATER.EDU*
78-L	Music recorded at 78 rpm; collections, etc.	Doug Elliott	listserver	*LISTSERV@CORNELL. EDU*
University of Utah	information about music programs	Edward Asmus	distribution list; archives	*musepa@utahcca.bitnet*; also *musepa@cc.utah.edu*

Table 1. Additional network resources for musical research.

See the earlier article (Vol. 8, pp. 33-54) for communications formats.

Software Tools

Bach, The Font

Rhythmics

CWU Music Scores

Gandharva

The LIM Workstation

Common Music

Tantrum and *Justune*

WATER

ESAC Electronic Songbooks

Bach, The Font:
Inline Musical Graphics for Databases and Spreadsheets

Bach **2.3**

Bach, Version 2.3, is a shareware program designed to reproduce elements of musical notation found in manuscripts of Bach's time. The purpose of *Bach* is to support the intermixture of musical information and text within a single font (the text font is Roman). It may be used in word processing programs, databases, and spreadsheets running under Windows 3.0 and 3.1 (*Word*, *Ami Pro*, Informix *Wingz*). The fonts are of professional quality and may be displayed in the graphical environment of Windows and reproduced on laser printers. A close approximation to WYSIWIG effects can be achieved without the use of Adobe's *Type Manager*. A separate symbol editor, *Version Editor*, works with *Wingz*.

The elements of notation produced may be substituted for upper ASCII characters (positions 128-255). *Bach* provides support for notes, rests, clef signs, bar lines, time signatures, accidentals, ties, ornaments, and selected other symbols. Some ASCII assignments for ornaments and grace notes are shown below:

Ornaments										
	0255	0174	0251	0250	0186	0235	~	0252	0200	0202
	0245	0246	0203	^		0180	0184	0192	0194	0195	0193

Example 1. *Bach*: ASCII assignments for ornaments and grace notes.

The individual musical "characters" are designed not as isolated logical objects but as graphically combinable elements that can be sequenced, like letters, to create compound objects such as beamed groups of notes and long trills. Thus beams are supported by combining three or more "characters"—the initial note of a beamed group, the final note, and the intervening note(s)—from choices such as the following:

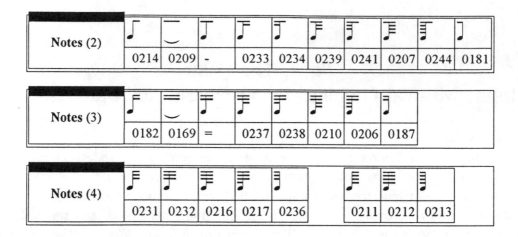

Example 2. *Bach*: ASCII assignments for particles of beamed groups.

The results that are achieved are aided by careful attention to placement within the available character space. Since *Bach* is intended only for use within text documents, it contains no down-stemmed symbols nor notes with a value of less than 1/64th. An in-line musical example may look like this: ♫ ♬ 　♩♯♯♫ .

Uses of the *Bach* Font

Bach was designed to address the need to insert facsimiles of musical notation into critical commentaries concerning manuscripts and variant editions of sources from Bach's time. A database of variant readings of manuscript sources of Bach's *Well-Tempered Clavier*, Volume 2, has been compiled under Informix *Wingz* for Windows. It includes the errors and variants found in roughly 130 extant manuscripts. The aims of this database project are to ascertain their origin, analyze individual readings, and ultimately to establish source filiation, including some assessment of the position of now lost manuscripts. The result of this work will be published as Volume II of my study *J. S. Bach's DAS WOHLTEMPERIERTE CLAVIER II: A Critical Commentary* planned for early 1994 [Vol. I was published in Leeds by Household World in 1993].

Example 3 shows the use of *Bach* in a study of amendments to MS 743 in the Royal College of Music, London. The top five rows locate the item. The next eight rows show the exact presentation of the information in eight manuscripts of the Altnikol tradition. Miscellaneous comments appear in the bottom row.

A auxiliary bibliography of reference materials concerning the music of Bach contains 12,600 items.

Movement	Pr.C	Pr.C	Fg.C♯	Fg.c♯
Bar	3	28	29	26
V,bt/pos	A,2–4	S,3–4	A(1; A2);T,3–4	S,3/1
Element	NV	rhy	rhy,NV	pitch
Spec.Loc	♩ ♩ [c']	♩ ♫ [a'' ab'']	♪♩ ♫ ♩ ♪××× [e♮'/c♯'/a♯']	♪♩ [a']
P 430	♩ ♩	♩ ♫	as above	rev: a'' → a'
msM24.B2	♩ ♩	♩ ♫ !	as above	a'
Konwitschny	♩ ♩	♩ ♫	♪♩ ♫ ♪× ♪×××	a'
P 204	♩ ♩	♩ ♫	as above	a'
P 402	♩ ♩	♩ ♫	♪♩ ♪/♩♪ [e♮'/a¹ c¹']	a''
RCM 743	♩[ ]♩ am	♩×♩[.] am ← ♩Bl	×♩♪/[♫♫]♩ [f×'/e' c¹' d¹' e'] add DBl	♯scr: a''→a'
Poel.33,2	♩ ×♯× !	♩×♫	♪×/♫♫ [a¹ c¹' e♮' f×']!	a''
PM 5697	♩.	♩ ♫	♪♩ ♪/♩♪ ♩ (or ♪♩ ♩) [f×'/a¹ c¹' e♮']	a''
additional comments	It maybe related to the notation of S where CHG SYS caused the split of a dotted minim.		RCM 743's variant reading is unique, which is probably filled in a vacant space without making reference to authentic text. The variant in other MSS of A is most likely caused by vague notation in S where flag / beam and dot were not clearly written.	This revision is carried out together with the alto.

Movement	Pr.D	Pr.D	Pr.D	Pr.d♯
Bar	4	28	42	16
V,bt/pos	A,3–4	S,4/3	S(A),3–4	S,1
Element	slurs	NV (stem,flag)	slur	rhy
Spec.Loc	♫♫ [a' g' g' f♯']	♩ ◡ [c♯']	♫♫ [a' g' g' f♯']	♫♫♫
P 430	^^	♪ ×♯◡	A: ^^	♯ok.
msM24.B2	^^ + S: ^^♯	♪◡	S: ^^; A: ^^	ok.
Konwitschny	^^	♪◡	A: ^^	ok.
P 204	◡◡ in S	trim: ♪ → ♩	S: ^^; A: ◡◡	♯ok.
P 402	^^ + S: ^^	××	no slurs	ok.
RCM 743	^^ + S: (^^) add' DBr	scr: ♪×'→ ♪× below S,4/5!	add' S: ◡◡; A: ^^ DBr	rev ← ♫♫♫♪
Poel.33,2	^^ + S: ^^	××	no slurs	♫♫♫♫
PM 5697	^^ + S: ^^♯	××	A: ^^	ok.
additional comments		It is significant that this note (stem) is not found in the related MSS (P 402, Poel and PM). The p.corr. reading is also found in P 1078 and VII.49736 (but without a tie before c♯')		This error may have stemmed from the way S was written unclearly.

Example 3. The use of *Bach* in comparing notational elements of eight manuscripts in the Altnikol transmission constellation.

Access to *Bach*

A shareware version for PCs is available by anonymous FTP from Indiana University. To retrieve a copy, use the procedure shown on p. 56 with these changes:

At the mainframe prompt: **ftp** *ftp.cica.indiana.edu*
At the **ftp>** prompt: **cd** *pub/pc/win3/uploads*

The filename is *bach-sw.exe*. This file, which is LZH compressed, includes *PostScript* Type 3 fonts and HP LaserJet II and III portrait fonts. A PC version with more extensive features and documentation is available at modest cost from the developer. A Macintosh version is under development.

In order to meet numerous requests for the creation of parallel sets of "music characters" that could serve to document sources and create critical commentaries for other repertories, collaborators who could assist in font design are now being sought.

Further information: Yo Tomita, Dept. of East Asian Studies, The University of Leeds, England; fax: +44 532/333472; e-mail: *chi6yt@sun.leeds.ac.uk*. The shareware version may be obtained by e-mail or by sending a diskette or $5 to Dr. Tomita. The full version is $25 or £11.50.

Peo Oertli-Kassim

Rhythmics 1.0

Rhythmics, Version 1.0, is a program for the notation and analysis of percussive music. It runs on the PC. Music is encoded in *RNS*, the *Rhythmics Notation System*. Such symbols as ●, ○, ■, □, /, \, and ✖ are used. Beats and pulses are tracked separately.

The program handles pitches to 20,000 Hz and scores of up to 6,000 measures. Symbol tables and help menus appear on the screen. A set of percussion fonts is provided. Printed output requires a PostScript emulator or printer. Sound output via the internal speakers of the PC is supported.

Released in 1993, *Rhythmics* has been under development since 1988. The origins of the representation scheme can be traced back to 1981. Documentation is in German.

Further information: Peo Oertli-Kassim, Rhythmics, Sonnenhofstr. 1, CH-8952 Schlieren, Switzerland; fax: +41 1/7303737. School and student discounts are available.

The CWU Music Scores Application Project:

Interactive Linking of Scores, Analyses, and Recordings

The Music Scores Application of the Library Collections Services Project, a joint research project of Case Western Reserve University in Cleveland, Ohio, and the IBM Corporation, consists of a collection of digitized images of complete scores from published editions scanned into and retrievable from a mainframe computer that can be linked to one or more commercial compact disc recordings to allow access to the audio simply by clicking on any on-screen score measure. The application can also display one or more pages of graphical analysis simultaneously with the score on a double-page monitor.

The analysis can be linked to the score pages to serve both as an overview of the entire piece (the pages of the full score turn to match the audio as it plays), and as an index to the score, which can be accessed by page and measure by clicking on any section of the analysis. [See the illustrations on the following pages.]

The application has been designed initially for instruction in music history, analysis, instruction, and applied music, but the ability for a user to author links between digitized graphic information and laser-read sources (CD, video, etc.) offers wide potential for a diverse group of teachers, researchers and students.

The Music Scores Application interface is designed completely from objects familiar to the user, and does not require the use of the keyboard. Learning time for the application is extremely short. The Music Scores Applications, one of several applications for classroom instruction included in the Library Collections Services Project, will be available on any workstation with access to the campus fiber optic network (CWRUNet). LCS is part of Case Western Reserve University's plan for its Library of the Future.

Two of the goals of the LCS Project, of which the Music Scores Application is a component, are (1) the establishment of online collections of fulltext books, music scores, and related materials and (2) the establishment of agreements with copyright holders as to the use of copyrighted materials in this new electronic environment.

Music Scores Application—left side of screen: image of page 32 from Bach's Partita No. 2 for Unaccompanied Violin. See explanation on the following page.

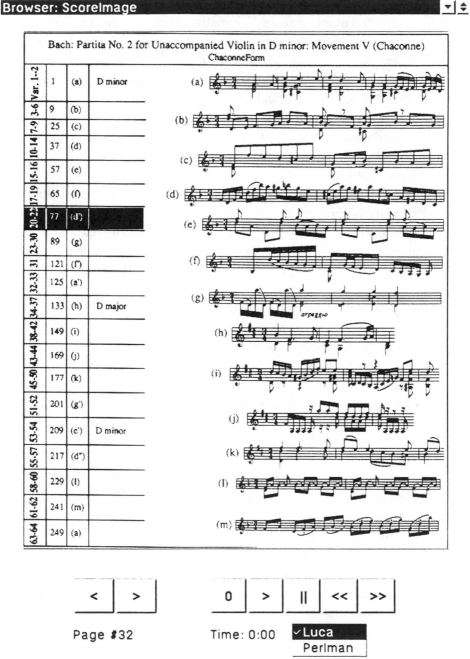

Music Scores Application—right side of screen: Sections of the work are listed by letter name on the left. Measure and section numbers are given in the columns on the left. The user clicks on the section or measure desired and an appropriate page of the score is displayed on the left half of the screen.

Score Access

The online collection of music scores is initially planned to number about 1,200 items chosen to meet the teaching needs of the Department of Music at Case Western Reserve University.   Users will be able to search online for these scores in traditional bibliographic fashion, or by data fields such as instrumentation, genre, date of composition, formal type, or historical period.   Once found, the score is displayed according to user preference.   Options include viewing one page at a time or viewing facing pages, non-consecutive pages, or even different scores simultaneously.

Graphic Analysis Links

A graphic analysis of the work may be displayed on the monitor simultaneously with the score.   The analysis provides both a formal overview of the score (the "forest" to help orient the user among the detailed "trees" of the full score notation) as well as an index to its important structural points.   Analyses are created in existing word processing, graphic, page makeup or other programs, and imported or scanned into the Music Scores Applications.

Analyses may be created and linked to any user, allowing a single score to be used, for example, by several different classes.   The analysis is linked section-by-section to the appropriate measure in the score at the author-user's discretion.   Clicking the mouse in any analysis section turns to the appropriate score page and highlights the measure at which that formal section begins.   The analysis may be continuously displayed as the pages of the score turn automatically to match the audio; analysis sections are highlighted as they are reached in the audio.

Recording Links

Any user may link the score measure-by-measure to any compact disc recording via the CD-ROM drive attached to the workstation.   User access to the recordings is achieved by double-clicking with the mouse in the desired starting measure, or by clicking the desired starting measure and then clicking the "play" button on the control panel.   Pages turn automatically to match the recording.   An unlimited number of recordings may be linked to the same score, allowing immediate and detailed comparison of different performances when multiple CD-ROM drives are available.   The ability to link Videodisc recordings to scores and analyses is now being developed.

Copyright Issues

The Library Collections Services Project is also addressing the issues of fair use of copyrighted materials in this new electronic environment.   The application controlling copyright matters, called Royalty Manager, has the following functions:

- To maintain a royalty/copyright database that includes information on license agreements, usage, etc.

- To maintain information about and report on electronic library holdings and users (subject to appropriate patron security procedures).

- To produce reports required by copyright holders and electronic library administrators.

- To produce files for billing and compensation.

Further information: Richard E. Rodda, Music Scores Application Leader, Library Collections Services, Baker Building, Room 6, Case Western Reserve University, Cleveland, Ohio 44106-7033, tel.: (216) 368-5888; fax: 368-8880; e-mail: *rxr10@po.cwru.edu*.

Rajeev Upadhye

Gandharva

Gandharva is a program designed to facilitate experimentation with the principles of Indian Classical music. It runs on the Macintosh II series and PC 286 and 386 micro-computers.

Gandharva uses one of the standard notation schemes in Hindustani Classical music, the Paluskar system of notation, which can be represented by ASCII text. The name of the raag, tala, tempo, and the lyrics, pitches, and durations are given. Durations, which vary markedly, are calibrated to show relationships to a fixed unit of time. The stored text can then be extracted to provide the foundation for elaborate musical compositions.

An intonation editor is provided. It supports retuning of the 12-note scale. *Gandharva* handles music over a three-octave range.

Further information: Rajeev Upadhye, Centre for Development of Advanced Computing, University Campus, Pune, Maharashtra, India 411007; tel.: +91 212/332461; fax: 212/337551; e-mail: *music@parcom.ernet.in*.

The LIM Intelligent Music Workstation

The Intelligent Music Workstation is the product of a five-year (1989-94) series of projects devoted to the development of a computer environment in which commercial products are integrated with custom modules built up in the framework of musical informatics research. The workstation has been developed at the Laboratorio d'Informatica Musicale (LIM) in the Department of Computer Science at the University of Milan. The project is sponsored by the Italian National Research Council.

Most of the modules run on the Macintosh family of computers. All are able to import and export Standard MIDI Files in the three formats available. Soundfiles are compatible with the Digidesign *SoundDesigner* format. A HyperText interface is provided to enhance operating simplicity and user interaction.

The Intelligent Music Workstation uses an open environment, so that musicians can add their own applications without encountering any difficulties arising from special formats of music data. No suitable coding format for the symbolic level has been identified. The modules described below—for score segmentation, music publishing, and transliteration of graphical and textual models into music—are limited to those which may be of interest to musicologists.

ScoreSegmenter

This system for the analysis of scores includes the following:

- tools for the study of tonal distances—Lerdahl and Jackendoff derivative methods, Bertoni-Haus-Mauri-Torelli operator methods, and a Kolmogorov complexity evaluation tool;

- tools for the transformation of the musical structures inferred by analysis tools; and

- tools for the synthesis of new scores obtained by means of transformed structures.

It supports MIDI execution of any musical structure (original, inferred, transformed, synthesized). Musical texts are encoded in a *DARMS*-like notation form. Common music notation, score printing, and a graphical user interface are supported.

Since the segmentation methods proposed in the Lerdahl and Jackendoff derivative approach and the Bertoni-Haus-Mauri-Torelli operator approach were not completely satisfying for analytical purposes, we have tried to define a more general approach for the segmentation of music texts. We are now able to segment fugues; models of other musical procedures will be formalized so that our segmenter will know their characteristics, too.

We are concurrently working on the description of formal methods for the automatic instrumentation of piano scores by means of a Ravel-like model derived from the analysis of the instrumentation of Musorgsky's *Pictures at an Exhibition*.

Electronic publishing of music

The definition of a minimum set of musical symbols which are sufficient for professional music publishing has been investigated. A digital music font has been implemented by METAFONT and customized on a ROM for a dot-matrix printer. A general approach to the automatic formatting of musical scores has been defined. A *DARMS*-like code for musical information has been formalized. It is suitable both for musical text formatting and for musicological analysis. A parser for this code has been implemented on a UNIVAC 1100/80 computer.

A software prototype allows the musician to format musical scores using digital music fonts, to use the mouse to pick up symbols from the fonts, and to put them into scores. The formatted scores are also translated into a *DARMS*-like notation, which can be used as input to the system for analysis mentioned above.

Data structures and information retrieval tools have been developed under Unix to manage a data base of musical scores stored on a CD-ROM. A joint project with the Conservatory of Music "Giuseppe Verdi" of Milan facilitates publishing of new editions of materials in the Noseda collection, a rich source of manuscripts at the Conservatory.

TEMPER

TEMPER is a program that transliterates graphic tessellations and literary texts into music. Music and graphic objects are related by means of tables of correspondence and rules that control both the spatial growth of graphic processes and the time growth of music processes. Graphic rules are the result of the analysis of M. C. Escher paintings. Music rules are referred to common music syntactic constraints.

In one early experiment the metric-rhythmic structure underlying the dialogue between Othello and Iago in Shakespeare's *Othello* was transliterated into music. It has been followed by experiments with passages from the works of Dante Alighieri, Ugo Foscolo, and Gabriele d'Annunzio. MIDI execution and score printing are supported.

In addition to the Workstation project, we are also engaged in a number of other computer-based projects. Two are:

• *The Piano*, a **CD-ROM**. The contents of the CD-ROM consist of a hypermedia volume about the instrument. Iconographic, audio, historical, and musicological materials are based on the unique collection of instruments and related iconographic, audio, and textual documentation available at the Accademia del Fortepiano in Florence.

• **Instrument modelling**: a modular environment will enable the musician to build imaginary instruments by recombination of traditional features such as strings, bows, frets, bellies, bridges, and so forth.

References

Ballista, A., E. Casali, J. Chareyron, and G. Haus. "A MIDI/DSP Sound Processing Environment for a Computer Music Workstation," *Computer Music Journal*, 16/3 (1992), 57-72.

Bertoni, A., G. Haus, G. Mauri, and M. Torelli. "A Mathematical Model for Analyzing and Structuring Musical Texts," *Interface* 7/1 (1978), 31-43.

Haus, G., and P. Morini. "*TEMPER*: A System for Music Synthesis from Animated Tessellations", *Leonardo*, 25/3 & 4 (1992), 355-60.

Haus, G., and A. Rodriguez. "Formal Music Representation: A Case Study: the Model of Ravel's Bolero by Petri Nets", in *Music Processing* (Computer Music and Digital Audio Series), ed. G. Haus. Madison, WI: A-R Editions, 1993.

Haus, G., and A. Sametti. "SCORESYNTH: A System for the Synthesis of Music Scores based on Petri Nets and a Music Algebra" in *Readings in Computer Generated Music*, ed. Denis Baggi (IEEE Computer Society Press, 1992), pp. 53-78.

Haus, G., and A. Stiglitz. "A Software Tool for the Functional Performance of Music," *Proc. SISEA* [Second International Symposium on Electronic Art], Groningen, Holland, 1991.

Further information: Goffredo Haus, Scientific Director, Laboratorio di Informatica Musicale, Dipartimento di Scienze dell'Informazione, Università degli Studi di Milano, via Comelico, 39, I-20135 Milan, Italy; tel.: +39 2/55006.338 or .382 or .380; fax: +39 2/55006.373; e-mail: *MUSIC@IMIUCCA.CSI.UNIMI.IT*.

Software availability: A suite of fourteen programs including *ScoreSegmenter* and *TEMPER* and a library of import/export routines for Standard MIDI Files (1.0) is available to non-profit organizations. There is no charge for the software *per se*, but a charge of approximately $185 for writing of the files to ROM and handling is made; additional postage charges and taxes may be applicable. Information on this service is available from CD-Express srl, attn. Agostino De Andreis, via Maroncelli, 9, I-20143 Milan, Italy; fax: +39 2/012364.

Heinrich Taube

Common Music

Common Music is a sound management program that runs on the Macintosh, NeXT, Sun, and Silicon Graphics workstations. *Common Music* is based on Common Lisp. It contains a composition editor called *Stella* that supports a non-Lisp style of interaction with the system. *Common Music* does not need a DSP [digital signal processing] chip to produce music. It can output to most generally available sound synthesis programs such as *Csound*, *Music Kit*, MIDI, and *Common Lisp Music*, which may or may not use a digital signal processing chip.

It is currently being ported to the Windows environment on 486 PCs. It may also be ported to the 486/*Linux* environment [*Linux* is a shareware PC version of Unix.] On the NeXT and Mac, it is possible to generate MIDI output in real time directly to the MIDI drivers, and direct-to-soundfile for Common Lisp Music. Implementation of a real-time connection to the Music Kit for NextSTEP as well as MIDI real time on the Silicon Graphics workstation are under development.

The source code to *Common Music* is free. The latest version of it may be obtained through anonymous FTP from either *ccrma-ftp.stanford.edu* or *ftp.zkm.de* in the file */pub/cm.tar.Z*.

Further information: Heinrich Taube, Zentrum für Kunst und Medientechnologie, Ritterstr. 42, D-7500, Karlsruhe 1, Germany; e-mail: *hkt@zkm.de* and *hkt@ccrma.stanford.edu*.

Tantrum and Justune:
Two Tools for the Study of Temperament Anomalies

Because musical pitch classes repeat at the octave, the gamut of pitch classes may be conveniently arrayed around a circle (as in CCARH's mandala—see the cover or frontispiece). Where, precisely, on the circle should the pitch classes be placed in order to accurately represent their tuning? This depends on the temperament being represented. For equal temperament, the 360° is divided equally into twelve 30° sections; each section represents the twelfth root of two ($2^{1/12}$)—the equal-tempered semitone.

For just-tuned intervals (those in which the frequencies of the pitches are related by whole-number ratios), however, the angles are not exact multiples of 30°. A just-tuned major third (a frequency ratio of 5:4), for example, is not 120°, but about 126.4°. A just-tuned perfect fifth (a frequency ratio of 3:2) is not 210°, but about 210.58°. Let us imagine a geometrical construction containing the angles represented by the previously mentioned just-tuned intervals.

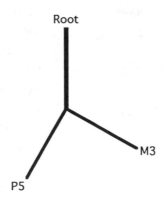

Figure 1. Angles representing the root, major third, and perfect fifth in just intonation.

In Figure 1, we see three spokes radiating from a common hub. One spoke represents the root. The other spokes represent pitches at the intervals of a major third and perfect fifth from that root.

If one adds a second set of spokes, with the same intervals as the first, but with the root of this second set aligned with the perfect fifth of the first set, then the diagram would be as follows:

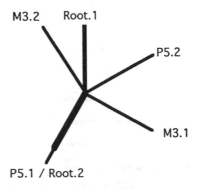

Figure 2. A second root-third-fifth set in just intonation: the fifth of the first set serves as the root of the second set.

Repeating this eleven more times, we return to the starting point—almost. The difference between a just-tuned perfect fifth (210.58°) and an equal-tempered perfect fifth (210°) has been multiplied twelve times; we're now about 7° off. This discrepancy corresponds to the out-of-tuneness of the final perfect fifth in the Pythagorean temperament (equivalent to about 23 cents, known as the *diatonic comma*).

*   *   *

The foregoing geometrical construction is the underlying metaphor used in two software tools designed for studying temperament anomalies: *TANTRUM* and *JUSTUNE*. In these programs, the positions of the endpoints of the spokes are shown in a magnified view, and the spokes corresponding to a root and the just-tuned intervals as measured from that root can be moved as a set, keeping the angles (intervals) constant.

In the *TANTRUM* display, many characteristic features of the temperament are visible at a glance. Figure 3 and the discussion which follows describe the mouse-based Macintosh version; the mouseless IBM/PC version differs in some details.

In this temperament, for example, we can see that the major and minor triads built upon E, A, and D are all perfectly in tune. In the triads built upon C, F, and B-flat, the major triad is perfectly in tune, but the minor third is very flat.

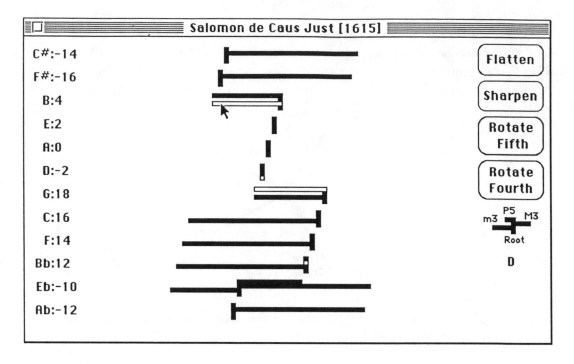

Figure 3. *Tantrum:* Triadic intervals in just intonation as described by Salomon de Caus [1615].

The tuning elements can be moved with the mouse. When the mouse is clicked on a tuning element, the element and all other instances of that pitch class are highlighted. In Figure 3, for example, the mouse has been clicked on the minor 3rd of the B triad, which is the pitch class D. As a result, this tuning element, as well as the root of the D triad, the fifth of the G triad and the major 3rd of the B-flat triad, have become highlighted. If the mouse is dragged, all four instances of this pitch class will move. In this way, the entire effect of retuning D can be seen; all four triads of which that pitch class is a member will be affected.

In *JUSTUNE*, the number of pitch classes can be set to any value from 1 to 99, and up to six just (whole number ratio) intervals can be viewed at once.

TANTRUM is available in versions for either Macintosh or IBM/PC. *JUSTUNE* is available for IBM/PC. The IBM/PC program requires EGA/VGA and a color monitor.

Further information: Stephen Malinowski, 5876 Park Avenue, Richmond, CA 94805, USA; tel.: (510) 235-7478 or 769-7717; fax: (510) 769-1953; e-mail: *smalin@well.sf.ca.us*.

Eitan Avitsur
WATER: A Workstation for Automatic Transcription of Ethnic Recordings

The aim of this project, begun in 1991, is to provide a workstation for diverse types of analysis of ethnic recordings. In particular, *WATER* provides new possibilities for very fine pitch tracking. It further provides a specialized extended graphical notation. This will improve our ability to study areas that were almost impossible to study using conventional techniques. Among them are:

- the study of minute deviations in microtonality as they relate to style

- pattern matching and categorization techniques for defining and classifying significant micro-elements as they relate to a corpus and its style

- a careful study of harmonic spectra and timbre as they change over time within single notes and the entire chant.

The environment is intended to be a general purpose one that will also support more common types of study, such as statistical analysis of intervals and motivic materials.

Thus far we have converted monophonic recordings of ethnic music into MIDI files using an IVL Pitchrider 4000 MARK II. After some experimentation, we were able to capture continuous microtonal changes in pitch. Using Daniel Oppenheim's *D-mix* software, a high-level object-oriented environment for musical applications running on the Macintosh, we were able to examine the continuous changes in pitch. However, the views provided in *D-mix* are not sufficiently accurate for a critical study.

As a final stage we would like to develop special tools dedicated to the study of microtonal changes in pitch within the level of each note. We would like this presentation to go side by side with conventional notation. In order to do so a dedicated, high-level graphical user interface must be specially developed. This will be, in effect, an automated extended-notation system. A further goal is to develop techniques for the analysis of polyphonic ethnic music that is recorded on a multi-track machine (one monophonic voice per track). We believe that the most efficient way to implement this project is by extending the *D-mix* environment.

Further information: Eitan Avitsur, Bar-Ilan University, Department of Musicology, Ramat Gan 52900, Israel; e-mail: *F2A002@VM.IU.AC.IL*; also Daniel V. Oppenheim, Thomas J. Watson Research Laboratories, IBM, Yorktown Heights, NY 10598; e-mail: *music@watson.ibm.com*.

Helmut Schaffrath

The *ESAC* Electronic Songbooks

This series of publications includes DOS-formatted diskettes of melodies encoded using the Essen Associative Code (ESAC). Supported modes of listening—using a PC speaker, a synthesizer, or an Ad-Lib-compatible sound card—include equal temperament or any user-defined tonal system. Melodies can be transposed. Pitch and rhythmic attributes may be separate. Accompanying texts include all diacriticals for European languages; Hebrew and Cyrillic texts and Chinese Jianpu (cypher) notation are supported. All text material is indexed. The music can be viewed on the screen and may also be printed via *PCX* files. In addition it may be converted to Standard MIDI files.

Volumes currently available or in preparation include the following:

- *634 German Folk and Children's Songs*, ed. Helmut Schaffrath. 5 vols.
- *106 Asturian Songs*, ed. Helmut Schaffrath. Now available.
- *565 Evangelical Church Songs*, ed. Christoph Finke. 4 vols. March 1994.
- *100 Catholic Church Songs*, ed. A. Becker. April 1994.
- *430 Bach Chorales after Riemenschneider*, ed. David Halperin. Now available.
- *106 Australian Folksongs:* THE SONGS THAT MADE AUSTRALIA, ed. W. Fahey. April 1994.
- *129 Polish Folksongs and Dances*, ed. Eva Dahlig. February 1994.
- *300 Traditional Blues Melodies*, ed. W. Kueppers. May 1994.

Future releases include the music of Slovakia, Switzerland, Luxembourg, Finland, Sweden, Russia, Roumania, Bulgaria, Greece, Turkey, Georgia, and Israel.

A recent thesis which considers the use of the *MAPPET* software (which has supported the creation of the Essen databases) in Sicilian popular music is that of M. Piemontese, "Sperimentazione del *MAPPET* per l'analisi computerizzata di un gruppo die melodie popolari Siciliani" (Laureate thesis in ethnomusicology, University of Bologna, 1993).

Further information: Helmut Schaffrath, Universität Essen, FB 4 - Musik - Postfach, W-4300 Essen 1, Germany; e-mail: *JMP100@VM.HRZ.UNI-ESSEN.DE*.

Applications

Fingering in Elizabethan Keyboard Music

A Study of Conducting

Tempo Hierarchies

Further Readings

Aiding Authentic Performance:
A Fingering Databank for Elizabethan Keyboard Music

A new computer program, written in the *SPITBOL* implementation of the *SNOBOL4* programming language at Nottingham University, can determine an appropriate fingering for a piece (or passage) of English keyboard music of the period *c*.1560-*c*.1630, the so-called Golden Age of English virginalist music. The program operates on a databank containing an extensive selection of fingerings found in manuscripts of English keyboard music of this period, which extends from the earliest surviving manuscript of English virginalist music[1] to the close of the decade which saw the deaths of the three principal composers of English virginalist music, William Byrd (d.1623), Orlando Gibbons (d.1625), and John Bull (d.1628).

Central to the process is the assumption that within any school of composition it is legitimate to apply the fingering of a musical configuration in one composition to a comparable configuration in a second composition, even if this is by a different composer. The program presupposes that the same principles of fingering applied at this period to all keyboard instruments (*e.g.*, organ and virginals); it assumes, also, that although there may have been small discrepancies in the size of keys between individual instruments, these differences are unlikely to have predicated any departure from the accepted principles of fingering.

A Brief History of Fingering Practices

The adoption of suitable fingering for a piece of keyboard music has for centuries been recognized as an important aspect of musical performance on all keyboard instruments—organ, harpsichord, virginals, piano, etc. From the mid-sixteenth century onwards prominent musicians left clear indications that the choice of correct fingering was a prerequisite for tasteful keyboard-playing: the early eighteenth-century French composer and theorist François Couperin wrote that "the manner of fingering contributes greatly to good playing,"[2] while the composer and theorist Carl Philip Emmanuel Bach—son of the great Johann Sebastian Bach—writing about half a century later,

---

[1] London, British Library, Royal Appendix 58.

[2] "La Façon de doigter sert beaucoup pour bien joüer." See François Couperin, *L'Art de toucher le clavecin* (1716; enlarged edn. 1717), ed. P. Brunold, in Couperin's *Oeuvres complètes,* I (Paris, 1933), p. 27.

asserted that "more is lost through poor fingering than can be replaced by all conceivable artistry and good taste."[3]   Even the more liberally-minded theorist Michel de Saint-Lambert, who regarded fingering as an area of considerable license, was compelled to concede that "there are situations in which all harpsichordists use the same principle, because they have found from experience that this is the most practical thing to do."[4]

The system of keyboard fingering in use today evolved in the early nineteenth century and differs markedly from the systems used in the sixteenth and seventeenth centuries. (Early players, for instance, used the thumb and the little finger relatively rarely, thus resorting for much of their playing to only the middle fingers on each hand.) However, even within the Renaissance and early Baroque periods different views prevailed: Spanish and German musicians of the late sixteenth century held conflicting views, with the Spanish being more progressive than their northern counterparts. English keyboard players generally favored Spanish practices, which spread to Italy during the seventeenth century.

The choice of fingering for a piece of early keyboard music can have profound implications for a musical performance. Most obviously, it will influence areas such as phrasing and articulation; it may also govern the speed at which a piece can effectively be played. Occasionally, early fingering may suggest that an ornament should be inserted, and it may even provide evidence as to *how* a written ornament should be interpreted. It is clearly desirable, then, that performers of early keyboard music adopt fingering which is in keeping with the style and period of the music itself, rather than fingering which is based on more recent traditions.

Most keyboard music written before the present century was not provided with fingering indications by either the composer, performer, copyist, or publisher. However, much keyboard music from the sixteenth through the eighteenth centuries—including works by such prominent composers as William Byrd, Jean-Philippe Rameau, François Couperin, and Johann Sebastian Bach—does carry contemporary fingerings, sometimes in the composer's hand.   In many cases the fingering provided is comprehensive, although it is more often confined to selected passages within a composition. Some composers, such as Henry Purcell (d.1695), have left theoretical tables indicating their preferred fingerings for passages involving scalic movement.

---

[3] *Versuch über die wahre Art das Clavier zu spielen* (1753), ed. William J. Mitchell as *Essay on the True Art of Playing Keyboard Instruments* (London, 1949; 2/1951), p. 41.

[4] *Les Principes du Clavecin* (Paris, 1702). See Eta Harich-Schneider, *The Harpsichord: An Introduction to Technique, Style and the Historical Sources* (Kassel and St. Louis, 1954), p. 21.

The Databank

Of the 60 or so surviving manuscripts of English keyboard music of the late sixteenth and early seventeenth centuries, approximately half contain fingering indications; of these about ten sources are particularly important.[5] The databank of fingerings used for this project is drawn predominantly from these ten sources and consists entirely of melodic fragments, ranging from a few notes to several bars in length. The databank contains no chordal passages, for which relatively little contemporary fingering exists. Consequently, the program's value is for determining appropriate fingers for single melodic strands. Since the majority of fingerings from this period relate to the right hand, the databank on which the process relies has so far been restricted to music intended for the right hand.

The unusual juxtaposition of white and black notes on a musical keyboard fundamentally influences the way in which the program operates. In encoding the passage to be fingered and in encoding the databank *absolute* pitch can be disregarded; only the physical juxtaposition of black and white notes is crucial.

The passage of music for which appropriate fingering is sought in the present instance comes from the opening bars of a variation on a galliard by "Ferdinand Richardson" from the *Fitzwilliam Virginal Book*[6] and is shown in staff notation as Example 1:

Example 1. Opening of a variation on "Richardson's galliard."

---

[5] Peter le Huray, "English Keyboard Fingering in the 16th and early 17th Centuries" in Ian Bent (ed.), *Source Materials and the Interpretation of Music: A Memorial Volume to Thurston Dart* (London, Stainer & Bell Ltd., 1981), pp. 227-8.

[6] The *Fitzwilliam Virginal Book*, ed. J. A. Fuller Maitland and W. Barclay Squire, 2 vols. (London, 1899; repr. 1963), I, no. 7, p. 34; the *Galliard* itself is found as No. 6 of the manuscript. Ferdinand "Richardson" was an *alias* adopted in his early years by Thomas Tallis's pupil Sir Ferdinand Heybourne (*c*.1588-1618).

Since pre-classical music is notationally economical—lacking performance indications such as tempo and dynamic markings, and marks of articulation—the encoding of the music into alphanumeric data can be very straightforward. Each note is encoded as a discrete 4-character field. The encoded version of Example 1, or what we will call the target piece, is as shown in Example 2:

Example 2. Encoding of music shown in Example 1.

The explanation of this system is as follows:

character 1:	direction of movement from previous note
+	ascending movement
-	descending movement
[blank]	no pitch change *or* first note following a rest *or* first note of a composition

character 2 < = n>:	indication of pitch difference from the previous note
[blank]	first note following a rest *or* first note of a composition
0	repeated note (white *or* black)
1	white note to adjacent white note, *or* black note to adjacent black note, *or* white note to adjacent black note, *or* black note to adjacent white note but one
2	white note to adjacent white note but one, *or* black note to adjacent black note but one

character 3:	color of note
W	white note
B	black note

character 4:	**duration**, according to the *DARMS76*[7] encoding system, but with lower-case letters indicating dotted notes in order to preserve a consistent fixed-length field for every note
T/t	Thirty-second note (*demisemiquaver*)
S/s	Sixteenth note (*semiquaver*)
E/e	Eighth note (*quaver*)
Q/q	Quarter note (*crotchet*)
H/h	Half note (*minim*)
W/w	Whole note (*semibreve*)
D/d	Double-whole note (*breve*)

A rest in the data is indicated as "9800", and "9900" marks the conclusion of a composition. The databank itself is encoded in exactly the same way, but as a *five-*character field in which the fifth character represents the finger used.

The right-hand part is submitted to the computer in a file encoded in the manner just described, although it may more conveniently be entered interactively at a terminal if it is reasonably short.

The Search for Fingering Patterns

Proceeding from the beginning of this target piece the computer scans the databank for the presence of a passage involving an identical juxtaposition of black notes, white notes and durations. Since any single hand position will usually allow a phrase of several consecutive notes to be played, a corresponding window of six notes in the target composition is sought in the databank.[8] The success of this process is facilitated by the fact that the recurrence of musical phrases across music by different composers is not uncommon at this period, partly due to *cliché* formations within the repertory, as would be likely to be the case with any musical *lingua franca*. The fingering from the databank is then directly transferred to the target composition.

With the exception of the first pass, which chooses fingers for the first three notes of the target passage, each successful pattern-match decides the fingering for only one note, *i.e.* the *third* note of the six-note window in the target passage. This is more easily explained in Example 3, where the first bar of the target passage is shown in its entirety

---

[7] *DARMS* = Digital Alternate Representation of Musical Scores. The existing manual documentation by Raymond Erickson (*DARMS. A Reference Manual*, New York, 1977) was compiled on the basis of a conference held in 1976. A chapter on *DARMS* will appear in E. Selfridge-Field *et al.*, *A Handbook of Musical Codes*, forthcoming.

[8] The choice of six notes as the size of the window is conceded to be arbitrary.

on the top stave. The numbers in the left-hand margin indicate the number of the pass through the data, with the large notes comprising the six-note window being sought, and the fingering resulting from that particular pass through the databank. In Window 1, for instance, Notes 1-6 are sought, and, when found, determine the fingering for Notes 1-3; the second pass seeks Notes 2-7, from which the fingering of Note 4 is decided. (The fingering of the first two notes has already been decided by the first pass through the data.) Similarly, Window 3 seeks Notes 3-8 in the databank, and determines the fingering for Note 5.

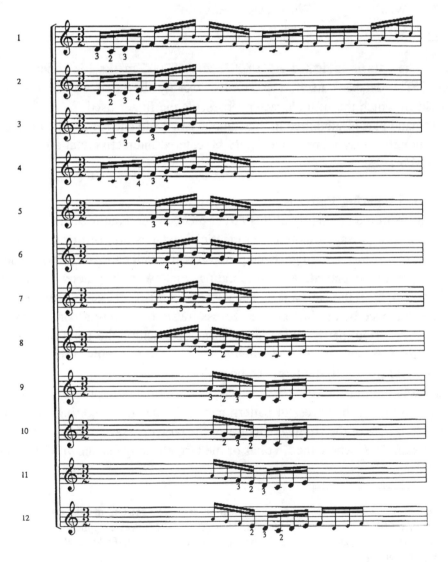

Example 3. Each staff represents a separate pass in which the six-note passage inspected is shifted by one position to the right.

Example 4 identifies those passages in the databank which were actually located by the twelve passes through the data, as illustrated by Example 3; the six-note window is shown in Example 4 in large notes, with the remainder of the measure shown in small notes. The references in the right-hand margin indicate that so far as the first twelve

Example 4. Passages in the databank that were located in the search shown in Example 3.

passes are concerned, the successful matches are found in one of three pieces—John Bull's *Preludium*,[9] the same composer's *Miserere*,[10] and Orlando Gibbon's *Praeludium*.[11]

Two observations are appropriate at this stage. First, when searching the databank for a given pattern, the computer takes the fingering from the *first* matching passage which it locates, and so the position of a piece early in the databank may mean that its fingering patterns are borrowed frequently. And, secondly, certain fingering patterns are particularly likely to recur in pieces in the same "mode" or key.

A matching six-note pattern will not always be located, as, for instance, in Window 4 of Example 4, in which case a *five*-note pattern—and failing that a *four*-note pattern is sought. A pattern as short as three consecutive notes is deemed acceptable where no longer pattern can be located; no shorter pattern would be valid, however, since it could not take account of both the note *before* and the note *after* that requiring to be fingered. As the program is currently structured, when no further patterns can be found the pattern-matching search turns toward similar—rather than exact—patterns, with the precise criteria of similarity being crucial to the program's validity. One way in which similarity is brought into play is by seeking a pattern which is identical so far as the configuration of black and white notes is concerned, but which involves shorter durations than those in the target passage. This is justified by the fact that a fingering pattern which is viable at one tempo is clearly no less practicable at a slower tempo, although the reverse is not true.

Examples 5a and b. Bars 3 and 5 of Bull's *Preludium*: fingerings of identical note sequences appear to obey rules of stress rather than of key sequence.

---

[9] Peter le Huray, *The Fingering of Virginal Music* (London, Stainer & Bell, Ltd., 1981), No. 3.

[10] *Ibid.*, No. 7.

[11] *Ibid.*, No. 5.

A fundamental requirement in all the pattern-matching processes is that the musical stress patterns of the target string and the located string correspond. In practice, this requires preserving the distinction between strong and weak sixteenth-notes (*semiquavers*). Examples 5a and 5b show, respectively, Bars 3 and 5 of John Bull's *Preludium*,[12] with the original fingering of the first two beats of Bar 3 corresponding with the last two beats of Bar 5; however, although the seven consecutive notes within the boxes are identical, the fingerings are out of phase, so as to allow the stronger fingers to be reserved for those notes which carry the greatest stress.

Sample Results

During execution the pattern-match attempts being made are reported to the terminal and/or written to a file for subsequent listing. The report for the opening of the target passage is shown in Table 1.

The target passage, as finally fingered by the computer, is shown as Example 6.

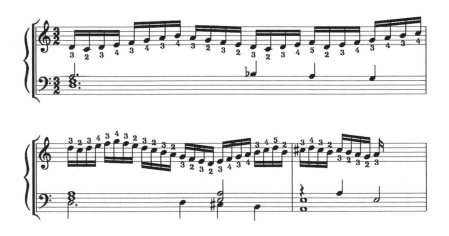

Example 6. The variation on "Richardson's galliard" as fingered by the program.

At program termination the incidence of all the six-note pattern-tables in the databank is listed, thus providing a quick check that a certain pattern which was unsuccessfully sought is not actually present in the data. Patterns 28-50 are shown as Example 7. The table can also be used to find the incidence of shorter patterns simply by using, say, the first three columns for a three-event match, the first four columns for a four-event match, etc.

---

[12] *Ibid.*, No. 3.

	Note	Identity	Finger	Data
§ Search for WS -1WS +1WS +1WS +1WS +1WS Searching DATA1 for opening pattern				
	1	WS	3	12
	2	-1WS	2	13
	3	+1WS	3	14
§ Search for -1WS2 +1WS3 +1WS +1WS +1WS +1WS Searching DATA1 for 6-note pattern				
	4	+1WS	4	15
§ Search for +1WS3 +1WS4 +1WS +1WS +1WS +1WS Searching DATA1 for 6-note pattern				
	5	+1WS	3	2
§ Search for +1WS4 +1WS3 +1WS +1WS +1WS -1WS Searching DATA1 for 6-note pattern Searching DATA2 for 6-note pattern Searching DATA1 for 5-note pattern				
	6	+1WS	4	1
§ Search for +1WS3 +1WS4 +1WS +1WS -1WS -1WS Searching DATA1 for 6-note pattern Searching DATA2 for 6-note pattern				
	7	+1WS	3	173
§ Search for +1WS4 +1WS3 +1WS -1WS -1WS -1WS Searching DATA1 for 6-note pattern Searching DATA2 for 6-note pattern				
	8	+1WS	4	174
§ Search for +1WS3 +1WS4 -1WS -1WS -1WS -1WS Searching DATA1 for 6-note pattern				
	9	-1WS	3	628

Table 1. Part of a search series.

28	+1BQ3	+1WH4	+9800	WS3	-3WS2	0WS4	1
29	+1BS3	+1WS4	+1WS5	-1WS4	-1BS3	-2WS2	1
30	+1Wq3	-1WE2	-1WE3	-2WE2	+2WE3	-1WE2	1
31	+1WE2	+1WE3	+1WE4	+1WE3	+1WE4	+1WE3	1
32	+1WE3	+1WE4	+1WE3	+1WE4	+1WE3	+1WE4	8
33	+1WE3	+1WE4	+1WE3	+1WE4	+1WE5	-1WE4	4
34	+1WE3	+1WE4	+1WE3	+1WE4	+1WE5	-2WE2	1
35	+1WE3	+1WE4	+1WE3	+1WE4	+1WW5	+9800	1
36	+1WE3	+1WE4	+1WE3	+1WE4	-1WE3	+1WE4	1
37	+1WE3	+1WE4	+1WE5	-1WE4	-1WE3	-1WE2	5
38	+1WE3	+1WE4	+1WE5	-2WE2	+1WE3	+1WE4	1
39	+1WE3	+1WE4	+1WW5	+9800	WH4	-1WE3	1
40	+1WE3	+1WE4	+2WE5	-1WE4	-1WQ3	-1WQ2	1
41	+1WE3	+1WE4	-1WE3	+1WE4	-1WE3	-1WE2	1
42	+1WE3	-1WE2	+1WE3	-2WE2	+9800	BS3	1
43	+1WE3	-1WE2	-1BE3	-1BE2	+1BQ3	+1WH4	1
44	+1WE3	-1WS3	-1WS2	-1WS3	-1WS2	-1WS3	1
45	+1WE3	-2WE1	+4WE5	-5WE1	+4WE5	-6BE1	1
46	+1WE3	-2WE2	+1WE3	-1WE2	+1WE3	-2WE2	1
47	+1WE3	-2WE2	+9800	BS3	-2WS2	+2BS3	1
48	+1WE4	+1WE3	+1WE4	+1WE3	+1WE4	+1WE3	6
49	+1WE4	+1WE3	+1WE4	+1WE3	+1WE4	+1WE5	4
50	+1WE4	+1WE3	+1WE4	+1WE3	+1WE4	+1WW5	1

Example 7. The number of occurrences (rightmost column) of fingering patterns 28-50.

The total number of different six-note finger patterns in the databank currently stands at about 620. The pattern table shows that the great majority of six-note patterns occur only once. They also show that the three most frequently occurring patterns are those given in Example 8:

Profile:						*Occurrences:*
+1WS5	-1WS4	+1WS5	-1WS4	+1WS5	-1WS4	20
-1WS3	-1WS2	-1WS3	-1WS2	-1WS3	-1WS2	17
+1WS3	+1WS4	+1WS3	+1WS4	+1WS3	+1WS4	16

As in:

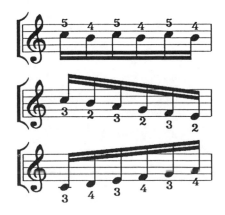

Example 8. The three most frequent patterns.

The popularity of these configurations is not at all surprising. Example 8a reflects the high incidence of fully written-out cadential ornamentation in some compositions, while Examples 8b and 8c reflect the heavy preponderance of scalic movement, especially in the context of modes which are less likely to exploit the black notes of the keyboard.

Controversial extensions of authentic fingering patterns have been excluded as far as possible. They cannot be totally excluded, however. Take the area of octave transpositions, for instance. It might reasonably be assumed that a certain musical pattern would be fingered in the same way irrespective of whether it is found in the center of the keyboard or whether it is found, say, nearer the upper extremity of the keyboard. Yet a fingering pattern may possibly involve more muscular strain at extremes of the keyboard.

Although the program has so far been used only for English keyboard music of the period *c.*1560-*c.*1630, it could be used without any modification for any repertory for which a sufficiently large body of previously fingered music already exists. Its use for fingering music played by the left hand would require only a new databank of music for the left hand. Its use for chordal music would be more problematical, however.

Further information: Dr. John Morehen, Department of Music, University Park, Nottingham, England NG7 2RD; fax: +44 602/514756; e-mail: *amzjm@vax.cc.nottingham.ac.uk*.

A Computer-Aided Study of Conducting

The aim of this research is to make the differences between performances the object of a reproducible musicological enquiry. The eventual aim is to be able to study interpretive style in the same way that musicology currently studies compositional style.

There are two problems: (1) the difficulty in the description of the differences and (2) the problem of memory: we can only listen to one recording at a time. We can eliminate the first problem by focusing our examination on the aspects of performance which are most quantifiable, namely tempo, tempo modulation, duration, and the quality which I call flexibility. We can eliminate the second problem if we use a computer.

Quantifiable Aspects of Performance

Tempo and tempo modulation have long been at the center of the debate about what constitutes "good" or "correct" performance. Conductors from Mendelssohn to Roger Norrington have argued that fast and steady tempos "let the music speak for itself" without "interference" from the performer, while Wagner based his entire interpretive theory on the idea that a performer *must* change tempo when the character of the music changes. From the objective/subjective debate between Toscanini and Furtwängler to the present discussions of historically accurate performance practice, tempo and tempo modulation remain central issues in the battle between performers and composers.

This initial study is limited to recordings of symphonies and all of the graphs presented here are from the expositions of first movements. An attempt has been made to collect and catalogue the first library dedicated to collecting *all* of the existing recordings for the following basic repertory of symphonies:[1]

---

[1] Simply cataloging in this way is something new, since almost all current discographies are of artists (a single conductor or singer for example). With the exception of the Mahler symphonies, there are no complete discographies published for any of these works. My sincere thanks to Barbara Sawka, Richard Koprowski, and Aurora Perez at the Stanford Archive of Recorded Sound for their help and support in this project.

Beethoven: Symphony No. 5
Beethoven: Symphony No. 9
Berlioz: *Symphonie fantastique*
Brahms: Symphony No. 1
Brahms: Symphony No. 4
Dvorak: Symphony No. 9
Mahler: Symphony No. 4
Mahler: Symphony No. 6
Mozart: Symphony No. 40
Schubert: Symphony No. 9
Tchaikovsky: Symphony No. 6

The Quantification Process

The most time-consuming step in the processing of collecting information about performance is to measure the duration between each beat, convert this number into a tempo measurement, and then store this series of numbers in a database. Using a program called *D-mix* (developed at the Center for Computer Research in Music and Acoustics, Stanford University, by Daniel Oppenheim), I tapped along with the performances and the computer recorded the time between each beat and then converted those numbers into tempo measurements. The result was a series of tempo measurements for each performance. These were exported to a text file/database.

The Analysis Process

Next the data is viewed in different ways. While *SAS/GRAPH* is really the only available program capable of dealing with enormous amounts of data (hundreds of performances with thousands of data points for each performance), I found that *DeltaGraph Professional* 2.03b (for Macintosh) was able to handle the files of single works, was easier to use, and produced better graphics. The figures shown here were produced with *DeltaGraph*.

CREATING TEMPO MAPS

The most basic plot is what I call a "Tempo Map." The horizontal or X-axis displays the measure, while the vertical or Y-axis displays the tempo for each beat. Each line represents a single performance, and the scale on each map is the same so that comparisons between figures are valid (see Examples 1a and b).

There is so much information here that each figure is restricted to a single performance. If we magnify the picture and focus just on the first statement of the second subject (*Andante*), however, we can place two performances on top of each other. We can also see that repeat performances by the same conductor, even years later with different orchestras, yield similar results not only in general approach but down to the details of individual notes and phrases (Examples 2a, b, and c).

In all these figures, we can see that there is a certain amount of human error in the measurements. Even limiting the measurements of duration between events to only one decimal place, there is error in both the perception and the transmission of the data to the computer keyboard.[2] While much of the "wiggling" of these lines is due to error in the measurements, however, the variation in the width of the lines in figures 1a and 1b is different. Karajan's performance is perceptibly more steady and more even on every level.

It is possible to eliminate some of this error by averaging. Figure 3 contains tempo maps for the first movement of the Mozart Symphony No. 40 in G Minor which use only the average tempo per bar (Examples 3a, b, c).

While there is still some wiggling which results from the error in the data, there is a noticeable difference in the angularity of each performance. It is also easy to see that the earlier performances divide the exposition of this symphony into tempo sections. We can clarify this by averaging again and looking only at the average tempo for each section (Examples 4a, b, and c).

COMPUTING FLEXIBILITY

At least two different kinds of tempo flexibility emerge from these graphs. One is the width or the flatness within a section, which I call the small-scale flexibility. The second is the gross difference between sections or the large-scale flexibility. The two, however, are unrelated and we can further explore this by adding a new measurement and reorganizing the data.

---

[2] The computer measures the time between events to as many decimal places as it needs. These measurements are converted to tempo measurements and then rounded to one decimal place. Control tests of the same performance are accurate to within $\pm$ 2 beats per minute. In other words a tempo measurement of 96 represents a tempo somewhere between 94 and 98.

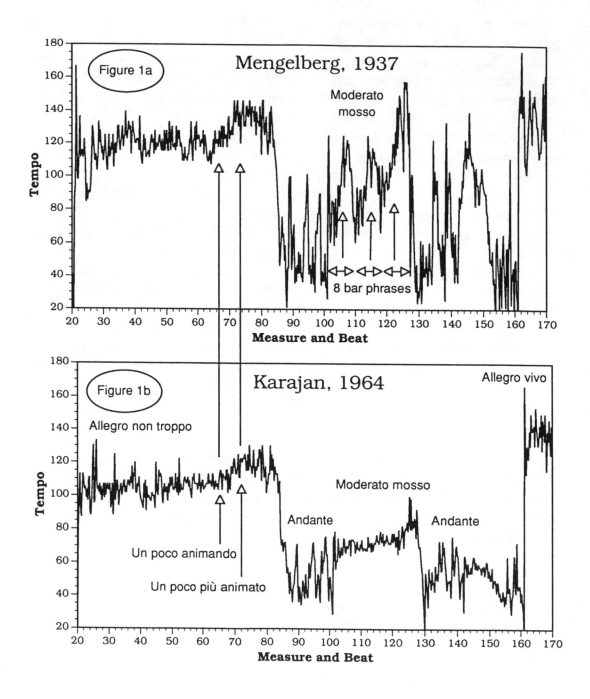

Examples 1a and 1b. Tempo maps of the first movement of Tchaikovsky's Symphony No. 6 in recordings by Mengelberg (1937) and Karajan (1964). Measurement is of tempo per beat.

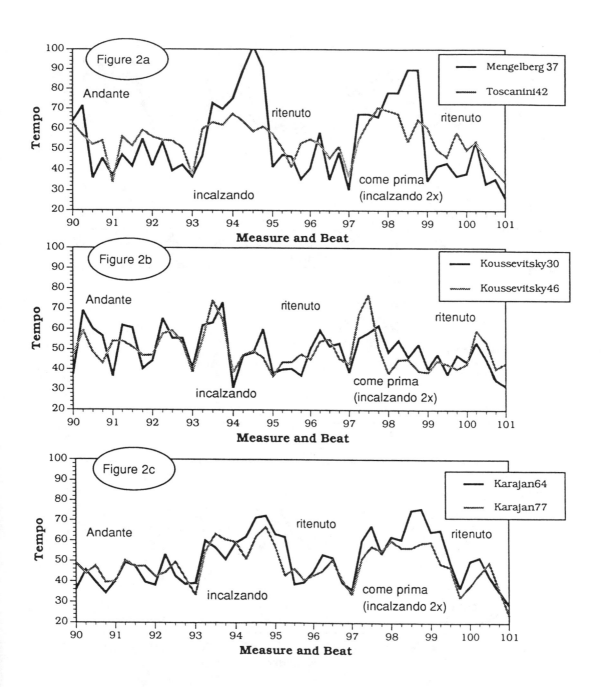

Examples 2a, 2b, and 2c. Tempo maps of the second theme of the first movement of Tchaikovsky's Symphony No. 6. The comparisons are of recordings (a) by Mengelberg in 1937 and Toscanini in 1942, (b) by Koussevitsky in 1930 and 1946, and (c) by Karajan in 1964 and 1977.

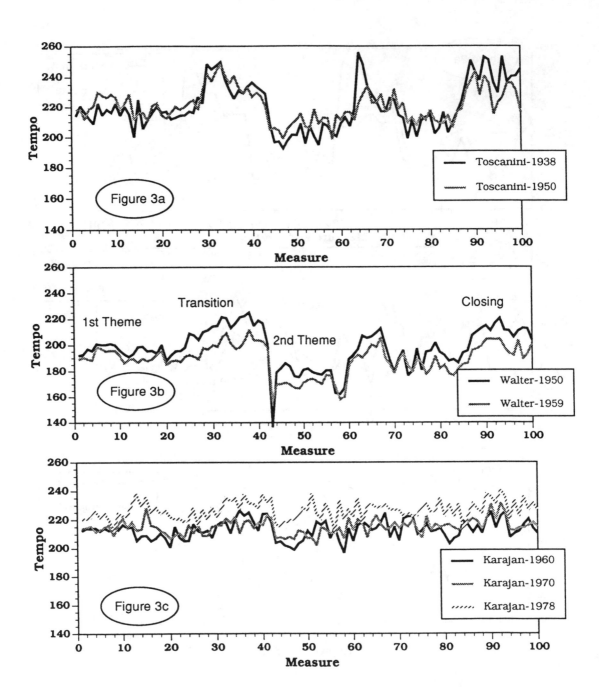

Examples 3a, 3b, and 3c. Tempo maps of the first movement of the Mozart Symphony No. 40 in G Minor based on average tempo per bar. Multiple recordings by (a) Toscanini, (b) Walter, and (c) Karajan are charted.

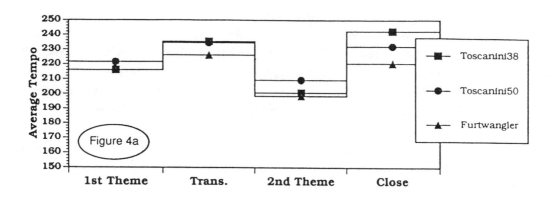

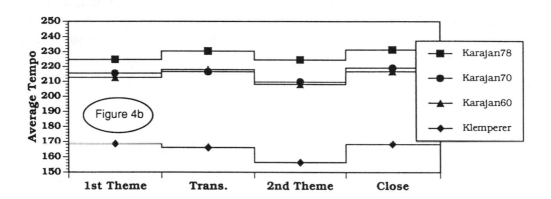

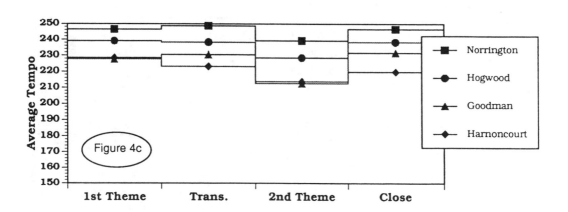

Examples 4a, 4b, and 4c. Tempo charts of the first movement of Mozart's Symphony No. 40 in G Minor based on average tempo per thematic section. Recent performances are shown to be faster but less varied than earlier ones.

Plotting duration against date (Example 5a) we see that the Beethoven Symphony No. 5 is gradually getting shorter. While notions that the repertory as a whole is speeding up or slowing down have been circulating for some time, there are in fact no overall trends. While some pieces are getting faster, others are getting slower and most show a consistent range. More important is where the piece is getting faster. We find from Examples 5b, 5c, and 5d that it is primarily in the second theme that the piece is losing time.

In addition we can measure the flexibility of the performance by comparing tempo directly to duration (Example 5e). In addition to sectional tempo changes, flexibility is a measure of the amount of acceleration or relaxation in a performance. The metronome line indicates what the duration would be if the orchestra stuck to the initial tempo unflaggingly, like a marching band. The average flexibility line is a simple linear regression. The Beethoven graph looks somewhat like we expect. Due to fermatas and retards, there is more relaxation than acceleration. In general the earlier performances are clustered around the outside of this graph, while the modern conductors all tend toward the average.

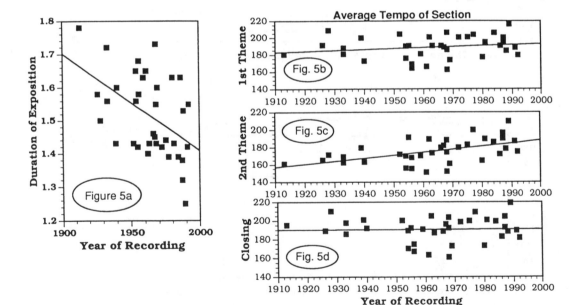

Examples 5a, 5b, 5c, and 5d. Tempos (averaged by section) in recordings of Beethoven's Fifth Symphony become faster over time, especially in the second theme.

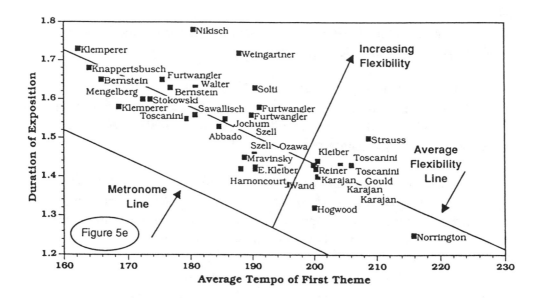

Example 5e. In recordings of Beethoven's Fifth Symphony average flexibility decreases as tempo increases.

Results

Evaluation of the visual data prepares the way for numerous observations and conclusions. A single example will suffice.

The current assumption is that Mozart specified no tempo changes in the exposition of Symphony No. 40 because he wanted none. While we might expect that all of the historical instrument performances are fast and steady, the assumption until now has always been that Toscanini was the father of this school of modern conducting.

Examples 3a and 3b, however, clearly demonstrate that both Toscanini and Walter shape the piece into tempo sections, while it is Karajan (Example 3c) who first begins to move toward a cooler, more modern approach. Walter and Toscanini, however, have very different approaches and the tempo maps accurately reflect those differences.

As can be both seen and heard, the Toscanini performances have more sudden shifts of tempo while the Walter performances present a more gradual and gentle play of tempo to indicate phrasing.

Walter's performances are smoother and more graceful than either Toscanini's or Karajan's. Note also how remarkably similar the different performances by the same conductor are to each other, regardless of the different orchestras involved or the passage of decades. It is hardly a great leap to suppose that the similarities are due to the presence of the same conductor. That is to say that we can find a tangible and fixed component of interpretive style to study in these tempo maps.

Conclusions

While research continues, some of the general conclusions which emerge from the study of different works include the following:[3]

- There are three often unrelated levels of flexibility: sectional, phrase, and bar. Sectional or large scale flexibility alters the tempo of an extended passage like the second subject. A smaller scale flexibility can occur on either the phrase or the bar level.

- Despite the rhetoric, the records of Toscanini and Furtwängler and all of the early conductors attest to Wagner's all-pervading influence on the practice of conducting; tempo fluctuation was an essential part of the conductor's job even for those who claimed to oppose it.

- While conductors from the same generation share certain traits, the earlier conductors each tend to remain somewhat unique, while the modern performances are more alike.

- The post-Karajan conductors tend to use less small scale flexibility, but often use more large scale sectional change.

- Even the most "improvisatory" conductors tend to retain a single conception and execution of the piece. It should be possible, therefore, to discover the characteristics of a conductor's style which are independent of any single work.

The final stage of this research is, therefore, the writing of an artificial intelligence program which will allow a computer to learn (as we do from these examples) what the style of each conductor is. The test will be to try to determine the conductor in a work which is unknown to the computer.

Composers, performers and theorists have argued for almost two centuries (since performers and composers began to be different persons) over what elements are and should be controlled by the composer and what elements are available for interpretive decisions. Within our own century the range runs from John Cage, who tried to release all control, to composers who use computers to control everything. This research will

---

[3] For the details of the initial findings see José A. Bowen, "Can a Symphony Change? Establishing Methodology for the Historical Study of Performance Styles" in *Der Bericht der Internationaler Kongress der Gesellschaft für Musikforschung: Musik als Text* (Kassel: Bärenreiter Verlag, 1993).

allow us to study not what should be changed, but what elements of the musical work *do* change, and clearly tempo and tempo modulation change. For each piece the history of "interpretation" is actually the history of the changing musical work.

References

Bowen, José A. "The History of Remembered Innovation: Tradition and Its Role in the Relationship Between Musical Works and Their Performances," *The Journal of Musicology*, 11/2 (Spring 1993), 139-173.

Bowen, José A. "Mendelssohn, Berlioz and Wagner as Conductors: The Origins of 'Fidelity to the Composer'," *Performance Practice Review,* 6/1 (Spring 1993), 77-88.

Bowen, José A. "The Conductor and the Score: A History of the Relationship Between Interpreter and Text from 1830 to 1880." Ph.D. dissertation, Stanford University, 1994.

Further information: José A. Bowen, Department of Music, Stanford University, Stanford, California, USA 94305; tel.: (415) 326-7110.

Guerino B. Mazzola

Establishing Tempo Hierarchies

Using a MIDI grand piano and a repertory of examples from Czerny and Chopin, we have successfully indetified tempo hierarchies. Musical time is determined to be a complex, ramified stratification of local tempo cells and thus qualitatively different from physical time (Mazzola and Zahorka).

The input of the score represents temporal material (sound events, barlines, pauses etc.) distributed in different parameter spaces. The various predicates and their domains of validity are described by predicative categories of local compositions (Mazzola 1990), a formalization of the structuralistic semiology as seen from the perspective of topos theory (Goldblatt 1984). The structure of the relevant "textual" predicates (analogous to Agawu's "universe of structure") is deduced from atomic predicative combinations.

As an application of this theory, we were able to achieve a precise implementation of the Lerdahl-Jackendoff theory of grouping structure as well as different metrical, motivic, and harmonical approaches. These results were quantitatively evaluated to yield analytical weight functions, the basis of analytical potentials.

NeXT workstations in the Multimedia Lab of Zurich University and in the Dübendorf office of the author are being used. The MathPalette is used as a linking tool between the *Mathematica* kernel and the NeXT developer tools. Presently, the class library of the structuring scheme is being designed on the basis of the predicative categories introduced by Mazzola (1993).

References

Agawu, Kofi V. *Playing with Signs*. Princeton: Princeton University Press, 1991.

Goldblatt, R. *Topoi*. Amsterdam: North-Holland Press, 1984.

Lerdahl, Fred, and Ray Jackendoff. *A Generative Theory of Tonal Music*. Cambridge, MA: MIT Press, 1983.

Mazzola, Guerino, and Zahorka, O. "Tempo Curves Revisited—Hierarchies of Performance Fields," *Computer Music Journal*, 15/2 (1993).

Mazzola, Guerino. *Geometrie der Tone*. Basel: Birkhauser, 1990.

Mazzola, Guerino. "Geometry and Logic of a Musical Performance." SNSF Report, 1993.

Further information: Guerino B. Mazzola, Projektgruppe für Fundamentale Forschung in der Musik, Wangenstrasse 11, CH-8600 Dübendorf, Switzerland; tel.: +41 01-8219856; fax: 01-8219851; e-mail: *gbm@presto.pr.net.ch*.

Further Readings:
Data, Software, Applications

Data and Representation:

Franze, Ulrich. "Formale und endliche Melodiesprachen und das Problem der Musikdaten-kodierung," *Musikometrika* 5 (1993), 107-49.

A discussion of features of ESAC [Essen Associative Code] and issues of music representation in related applications.

Samson, Chris. "*Notafile*." Typescript, London, 1993.

Notafile is a file format designed by Chris Samson, who proposes that it could serve as an interchange format for sequencing and notation information. Copies of the specification are available for £15 from Datamusic, 57 Cricketfield Road, London E5 8NR, England, UK; tel. and fax: +44 81/985 5268.

Document Delivery:

Desniaski, David. "Online Catalogs Available on the Internet," *Music Library Association Newsletter* 94 (Sept.-Oct. 1993), 1-14.

Sample telnet access and logon scripts for selected university libraries included in the CARL, Dynix, DRA, GEAC, Illinet, Innopac, Notis, and VTLS networks are provided in this article, which comments on perceived strengths and weaknesses.

Software:

Opren, Keith S., and David Huron, "The Measurement of Similarity in Music: A Quantitative Approach for Non-parametric Representations," *Computers in Music Research* 4 (1992), 1-44.

A program for measuring musical similarity is described. Opren's *simil* is an implementation of the Damerau-Levenshtein metric for calculating the edit distance between two strings. It works with data in the *Humdrum* representation scheme devised by Huron. Possible uses are explored through comparisons based on melodic interval patterns, rhythmic information, and a full range of information about harmony, melodic contour, and rhythm in combination.

Overill, Richard E. "On the Combinatorial Complexity of Fuzzy Pattern Matching in Music Analysis," *Computers and the Humanities* 27 (1993), 105-10.

Examines procedures for matching strings of three ± one pitches provided by tools for Approximate String Matching as used in genetics, speech processing, and text correction.

Tomita, Yo. "The Spreadsheet in Musicology," *Musicus* (1992; forthcoming). See pp. 61-63.

Applications:

Dirst, Matthew, and Andreas S. Weigend. "Baroque Forecasting: On Completing J. S. Bach's Last Fugue" in *Predicting the Future and Understanding the Past*, ed. A. S. Weigend and N. A. Gershenfeld (SFI Studies in the Sciences of Complexity, Proceedings, XVII, Addison-Wesley, 1993), pp. 1-25.

A data-driven approach to completion is contrasted with a rule-based one. Statistical methods are used to characterize the data set, which appears to consist of MIDI key numbers. Contrapunctus XIV and some completions are available by FTP [*ftp.santafe.edu*: see the directory *pub/Time-Series/Bach*].

Gottschewski, Hermann. "Tempoarchitektur—Ansätze zu einer speziellen Tempotheorie oder: Was macht das "Klassische" in Carl Reineckes Mozartspiel aus?", *Musiktheorie* 8/2 (1993), 99-117.

Explores ideas discussed in "Graphic Analysis of Recorded Interpretations," in *Computing in Musicology* 8 (1992), 93-6; in the author's recent dissertation (Albert-Ludwigs University, Freiburg); and in Vol. 11 (*Interpretation*) of the *Neues Handbuch der Musikwissenschaft*, ed. Carl Dalhaus (Laaber: Laaber-Verlag, 1992), 318-9.

Theories and Models:

Analyse et modèles, a special issue of *Analyse Musicale*, 22 (Février 1991). Subscription information: Revue Analyse Musicale, 10, rue Chabanais, 3me étage, 75002 Paris, France.

This thematic issue of the review includes a number of articles of interest in computer assisted analysis. Among them, "L'Invention à deux voix n° 1 de J.-S. Bach: Essai de modélisation informatique" by Marcel Mesnage and André Riotte (pp. 46-66) illustrates a systems-based approach to motivic generation of the kind used in Bach's invention. A valuable bibliography concludes Bernard Vecchione's consideration of "Musique et modèles: Vers une typologie des modèles en musique," pp. 13-29.

Howell, Peter, Robert West, and Ian Cross. *Representing Musical Structure*. London and San Diego: Academic Press, 1991.

This carefully conceived collection of essays focusing on cognitive approaches to musical analysis is subdivided into two main parts: "Structure as Subdivision" and "Structure as Constraint." It is introduced by an essay on "Musical Structure and Knowledge Representation" by the three authors. Here they discuss the relationship between the two views of structure. The book is well edited and contains a wealth of procedural information that could be of value in computer-aided studies.

General Interest:

Nuñez, Adolfo. *Informatica y electronica musical*. Madrid, 1993. ISBN 84-283-1853-0. Published by Editorial Paraninfosa, Magallanes, 25, 28015 Madrid, Spain; tel.: +34 1/4463350; fax: +34 1/4456218.

This comprehensive introduction to musical informatics includes chapters on hardware and software and principles of their use, psychoacoustics, sound sampling and synthesis, melodic generation, ear-training exercises, and procedures borrowed from artificial intelligence. It is thoughtfully illustrated and clearly explained. It should remain useful in Spanish-speaking classrooms and home studios for a long time to come. A Spanish-English dictionary of terms is provided.

Optical Recognition

A Survey of Current Work

An Interactive System

Recognition Problems

The Issue of Practicality

Optical Recognition of Musical Notation:
A Survey of Current Work

Optical recognition of music—the machine acquisition of intelligent information through the correct interpretation of an electronically scanned image—is widely viewed as an important area of technical research. It is also an immensely difficult one. This explains why it was not until this year that the first commercial program appeared. Although research on OMR can be traced back to the work of David Prerau at M.I.T. more than 20 years ago, a large number of research efforts have been launched and nurtured over the past five years. Much of the literature they have generated is found in publications on image processing. The groundswell of recent interest is affirmed by the establishment in 1993 of two electronic discussions of optical recognition.[1] Some practitioners claim that the craft of optical recognition stands approximately where software for music notation stood ten years ago.

Vis-à-vis the additive process of composing musical notation, the general principle employed in most systems for OMR is one of subtraction. Removal of selected graphical elements up to the point where residual objects can be identified is the intermediate goal. Objects that can be isolated are much more likely to be identified correctly than those that cannot. More so than in music printing, the steps in the recognition process are unpredictable in number and nature.

First CCARH Survey

Numerous projects in this field have been reported in *Computing in Musicology* since 1987 [a list of previous reports is given on pp. 117-8]. Believing that it was time to introduce a systematic survey of the numerous and diverse efforts that are known to exist, we distributed a survey concerned with general aims and accomplishments to 36 OMR developers. One measure of the difficulty of the undertaking is that only six groups re-

---

[1] News about research related to optical recognition in general is circulated by Karl Tombre, INRIA Lorraine / CRIN-CNRS, Post: Batiment LORIA, BP 239, 54506 Vandoeuvre CEDEX, France, or 615 rue du jardin botanique, BP 101, 54602 Villers CEDEX, France; tel.: +33 83/59.20.71; fax: +33 83/41.30.79; e-mail: *Karl.Tombre@loria.fr*. Martin Roth [*cf.* p. 145] maintains an electronic discussion [*omr@ips.id.ethz.ch*] of recognition of musical notation.

turned detailed reports on their current work. Some researchers reported briefly that they did not feel that their work was far enough progressed to warrant an official report. A few regarded some of the information sought as proprietary.

For our part, we discovered that constructing a survey for optical recognition is a daunting task. Although some of our questions were intended to facilitate comparison, we learned that it is difficult, and at the present time probably unwise, to make them. The reasons why this is so are themselves instructive, particularly for potential users of optical recognition software. They are indicated in the following pages.

Approaches and Problem Types: A General Introduction

There are myriad approaches to optical recognition. Each one is guided by a different view of the most significant obstacles to recognition and the most efficient available means of addressing general problems of optical recognition.

1. Conceptual Issues

An overriding problem of interpretation is that of distinguishing foreground from background. We normally think of a musical score as a two-dimensional object, but it is actually interpreted cognitively as one of three dimensions. The third dimension consists of non-sounding cues to interpretation, such as staves and systems. For this reason, many systems begin with the removal of staff lines, which form a complicating visual background, in order better to reveal the foreground of notes, stems, and beams.

The adage that what is easy for human beings is difficult for machines is nowhere more true than in optical recognition. White notes are harder for most systems to identify than black notes because they contain very little visual matter. Contextual information is problematic: a dot of prolongation and a dot of articulation (staccato) cannot be distinguished by shape or size; they must be distinguished contextually. When it comes to interpreting the images captured, recognition programs must do a lot of the same bookkeeping required in music printing programs to interpret items correctly. Pitch interpretation is dependent on the clef in use, duration may be dependent on metrical signature, and so forth.

2. The Basic Process

The main steps in the process of music recognition are (a) capture of the image as a bitmap, (b) editing of the image to facilitate correct interpretation, (c) conversion of bitmap to a code (such as MIDI, *DARMS*, or *SCORE*) representing musical information, and (d) translation of the code to an application producing sound or printed musical notation.

3. Factors Relating to the Work Environment

The competence of the result and the ease with which it is obtained can be influenced by many factors—(1) the hardware, operating system, and software environment in use, (2) the graphic quality of the material scanned, (3) the complexity of the music, (4) the format to which conversion is sought, and (5) the efficiency of the applications program used to complete the recreation of the music.

(1) For programs implemented on the PC, acquisition times on a 486 will be significantly faster than those on a 386 but not necessarily the same from machine to machine, on which hardware components and operating setups may vary. Machine speeds have a significant effect on program performance. Programs implemented on some Unix workstations may have some inherent advantages conferred by specific resources for image capture and editing. The workstations themselves normally have much larger screens and higher screen resolutions than PCs or Macs, traits that are valuable in the editing of images.

(2) Many prototype programs of the past were designed to work only with single parts on one staff. Most current programs concentrate on music for not-too-large instrumental ensembles; many exclude keyboard music because of its often complex textures. We know of no program that attempts to capture text underlay in vocal music. Most do not attempt to capture other text elements, such as tempo indications. Users of recognition software must expect to supplement the material captured automatically with additional information if they wish to create performing materials.

(3) Intelligent scanning programs of the present time usually do not attempt to replicate completely the image of the original. Instead they try to capture selected attributes of musical information. Sound-out programs attempt to capture pitch and duration. Depending on the repertory selected, print-out programs may need to capture a significantly greater number of elements of information—slurs, stems, beams, articulation marks, dynamics, and ornaments.

(4) The time required to correct scanning errors will depend not only on the level of accuracy of the automatically acquired material but also on the nature and efficiency of the applications program into which the material is read, not to mention the user's facility in using it. While support for notation output is inherently more demanding than that for sound output, most programs intended to produce printed output from scanned material support only a finite number of the additional elements—stems and beams, perhaps, but not slurs. The number of attributes supported characteristically increases as the program grows in overall competence.

(5) There are no uniform measures of efficiency in the evaluation of applications programs. Some relevant issues are raised in the article "How Practical is Optical Music Recognition as an Input Method?" (pp. 159-166).

Problem Categories

Those involved in the development of programs for recognition of music tend to make decisions about all of the above items at the outset of their work. They spend much of their subsequent research time trying to address problems presented by the graphical image itself. These can be grouped into three categories—visual surface problems, object recognition problems, and problems of music representation.

1. Visual surface problems

Figure 1. **Surface imperfections**: skewing and ambiguous positioning (uppermost note).

Most visual surface problems result from imperfections in the printing. Given that the optical acquisition of works printed in recent decades is likely to violate copyright, scanning researchers often select materials from the nineteenth century for training materials. This is the case with all of the illustrations in this section, which come from the Breitkopf und Härtel edition of Mozart's Symphony in G Major, K. 114, published in 1879. The erratic typography shown in our enlargements is characteristic of a great deal of printed music that is legally available for scanning.

Some common imperfections are rotation of staves so that staff lines are not exactly parallel with the edge of the page, variability in staff line thickness, and incorrect positioning (Figure 1). However trivial they may seem to the human eye, these irregularities can be quite debilitating to recognition software, which can usually accept small variations but only within clearly set limits. Respondents to our survey reported acceptance limits of skewed images within the range of 5° to 10°. The image in Figure 1 is the only example shown here that has not been rotationally corrected by at least 1°.

Other problems of the visual surface fall into two categories—missing information and superfluous information. Staff lines and leger lines that are not continuous (as in Figure 2) as well as objects that are incompletely drawn (*e.g.*, the half note in Figure 3) or incompletely filled (*e.g.*, notes on the downbeat in Figure 4) are all familiar problems of insufficiency in the visual image itself. In all of these examples small variations in notehead size and placement relative to stems and staff lines can also be detected.

Figure 2. Surface imperfections: note the broken staff line at the top right and the variable width of both staff- and barlines.

Figure 3. Insufficient information: the half note and the natural sign both lack closure. Compare the hypothetical white space in the half note with the actual white space bordered by the stem, the notehead, and the contingent flag in the tied octaves of Figure 4.

The problems caused by superfluous information, which cannot be filtered by recognition software unless anticipated, are less likely to be evident to users. The most common kind of superfluous information is dirt (Figure 5).

Figure 5. Superfluous information: dirt.

Figure 4. Flawed information: the eighth notes on the first beat are incompletely filled. Note the variable distance between the staccato dots and the notes to which they pertain.

Depending on where it occurs in relation to other objects, dirt can be misinterpreted to be almost anything. If one were attempting to read the blob in Figure 5, one might be tempted by its placement to consider it a dynamics mark of some kind.

Programs can also create superfluous information through the misrecognition of objects. In one of the ensuing examples (5a on p. 132), dynamics markings were interpreted as whole notes. Errors of this kind are common in the development stage, since the effort to be selective about which musical attributes to capture provides scope for a category of errors that would not exist if all elements could be reliably captured.

2. Object Recognition

Optical recognition software in general utilizes a wide range of diverse approaches. One approach is to bound specified areas in a hypothetical box and make inferences from box sizes and shapes. If one were always scanning material from the same typographical source, such as a particular press that always worked with the same font and the same size staves, one might attempt to make templates for the various objects and match captured objects to the templates. Most situations are not so simple, and various methods developed in artificial intelligence are employed.

Problems of object recognition vary somewhat with the nature of the approach. Some approaches are better suited to large features, such as slurs and beams, others to small features, such as stems and flags. Reliable interpretation for replication of printed material will obviously require equal competence in the treatment of both ranges. This is the kind of success that remains elusive.

Problems that are common to most approaches include inconsistencies of size, shape, and presentation as well as those of superimposition. In all of these categories some confusing situations conform to the accepted grammar of musical notation and others occur by accident.

A. INCONSISTENCIES OF SIZE

An intended inconsistency of size occurs in the case of a grace note. A program that tries to identify objects by shape only might have trouble distinguishing a grace note or a cue note from an ordinary note. It can be filtered out by its size, providing that the surround area is not too noisy or too dirty. However, when one filters by size, then the erratic nature of page composition can muddle the result. In older scores that are, from a copyright perspective, appropriate for scanning, stem lengths and beam widths are likely to be variable (Figures 6a and 6b).

Figure 6a. Compare the stem lengths in this passage with those in Ex. 6b.

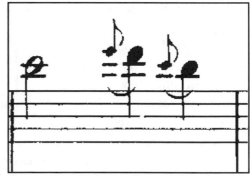

Figure 6b. Compare the stem lengths with those of Ex. 6a.

B. INCONSISTENCIES OF SHAPE AND PRESENTATION

Some intended instances of inconsistency in presentation would be the note centered on the staff line vs. the note centered on the space. When multiple beams cross multiple staff lines, many kinds of unpredictable shapes can result, especially since the angle of tilt in the beams is variable and the overlay created will depend on the vertical placement of the associated notes. This creates an unfortunate but accepted area of difficulty for visual interpretation. However, when such objects as rests and fermatas are erratically aligned in a score, a recognition program must search a relatively large area in order to locate and identify them. Clef signs, meter signatures, and quarter-note rests were frequently cited as problems because of wide variations in graphic design.

Figure 7. Superimposition: slurs touch noteheads. Note also that the flag of the first eighth note crosses a leger line.

C. CONTIGUITY AND SUPERIMPOSITION

Even when the quality of the original material is superb, the contiguous placement or Superimposition of objects presents serious obstacles to recognition. Slurs are especially troublesome. A slur crossing a stem (Figures 1, 6a, 6b) may be tolerated, but a slur touching a note (Figure 7) or crossing a dynamic marking creates apparent objects that will not be found in a graphic lexicon.

3. Problems of Music Representation

A generation of researchers have explored the anomalies of representing Western art music in common music notation without exhausting all the aberrations or describing them systematically. It is not the task of optical recognition research to do so, but since recognition software produces files for the reconstruction

Figure 8. Issues in music representation: half notes and quarter notes share common stems.

of musical scores and sounds, it is inevitable that from time to time problems of musical representation will need to be addressed. Global problems such as the realization of grace notes and the separation of tracks in keyboard works may not interfere often if the intended output is specifically for sound or for notation. Local problems are more likely to be troublesome. In Figure 8 we show one—an instance in which multiple objects (notes of diverse durations) share common parts (here stems) in an unlikely way.

Such examples interfere with a grammatical approach to object recognition, since in its graphic presentation the underlying logic of notation is beset on every side with exceptions of an unpredictable nature. Additionally, recognition programs may be confused by objects not intended for capture. One developer cited guitar chords as an example: they are hard to ignore because of parallel lines and black circles.

4. Partial Solutions

Approaches to optical recognition have varied widely over the years. Early efforts at text recognition often used *template-matching*. Since this depends on matching specific fonts at exact sizes, its value is severely limited in handling typographically diverse materials. Recognition by *geometrical analysis* of graphic features such as lines, angles, orientations, and curvatures of scanned objects is based on algorithmic matching. This approach overcomes the problems of exactness encountered in template-matching but elicits new areas of confusion in attempting to distinguish, for example, between b's and h's, l's and 1's, or O's and 0's.

The optical scanning of music cannot build entirely on these approaches, because the symbols used in musical notation are so much more numerous, their visual grammar so much more complex, and their meanings sometimes determined by contextual clues, as the previous figures have demonstrated. One technique is that of bounding groups of objects, such as a series of eighth notes connected to a common beam, and defining the contents hierarchically from most to least comprehensive. The demarcated area is called a *bounding box*. Researches have explored foreground-background separation (*i.e.*, removing the staff lines to expose the notes), background enhancement, tests of identity by rotation and/or slanting of objects, and a host of other image-processing techniques. In one enterprise, additional staff lines are hypothetically projected to assess the height and depth of objects above and below the staff. In another, the staff grid is not inspected along the whole of its horizontal length; instead the program sets the clef at the start of each line and assumes that it does not change along the way. This has obvious pitfalls for accuracy but saves processing time. Most enduring projects use a combination of methods to attend to the diverse problems encountered.

Some projects reported in recent issues of *Computing in Musicology* include the following:

- 1987: Bernard Mont-Reynaud, Stanford University; Unix environment.
- 1987, 1989, 1990, 1991: Nicholas Carter*, University of Surrey, UK—programming on Unix workstations and PCs; output to *SCORE* [notation program]. Now licensed to Coda Music Technology.
- 1987, 1990, 1991: Alastair Clarke, University of Wales, Cardiff, UK—programming on PC.
- 1987, 1990: Waseda University, Tokyo—one aspect of the WABOT musical robotics enterprise; limited number of symbols attempted; *SMX* [code] output
- 1990, 1991: William McGee*, Paul Merkley, University of Ottawa— programming on PC; original focus on syntactically simple medieval music [but subsequently broadened to common music notation]; output in *DARMS* [code] to *The Note Processor* [notation program]

- 1990: Dimitris Giannelos, ERATTO-CNRS, Paris—programming on Macintosh; focus on Greek Orthodox music; output to *Euterpe* [notation program]
- 1991: Ichiro Fujinaga, McGill University, Montréal—programming on Unix workstations and PC; output to *Nutation* [notation program for the NeXT]. Now licensed to A-R Editions.

*Starred contributors are among the respondents whose work is represented in the ensuing pages.

Seven Current Projects

The seven detailed responses we received concern three programs running on Unix machines and three on PCs. These can be briefly identified as follows:

Program	Respondent	Platform	Output format(s)	Application
AMSR	Kia-Chuan Ng	Unix	MIDI	sound
MidiScan	Christopher Newell	MS-DOS	MIDI	sound
MusicReader	William McGee	MS-DOS	*DARMS*, MIDI	printing, sound
NoteScan	Cindy Grande	Macintosh, MS-DOS	*NoteScan*, *NoteScan*	printing, sound
OMR	Martin Roth	Unix	*Lipsia*	printing
SAM	Elizabeth Botha	MS-DOS	*MOD*	sound
SightReader	Nicholas Carter	Unix	*SCORE*	printing

Since the difficulty of optical recognition varies tremendously with the kind of music scanned, our questionnaire listed ten kinds of pieces that would produce different problems. Respondents were asked to rate the difficulty of each. Their responses are indicated in Table 1. Note that the two examples we circulated—by Handel and Clementi respectively—represent a single printed part from an orchestral score and a simple printed score for piano. Respondents were also asked to rate the difficulty of capturing various kinds of musical objects. The results are indicated in Table 2. Note that most participants did not attempt to recognize all the object types in the set pieces.

A one-page description of each project follows these two tables of general information. In team efforts, the name of the respondent is indicated by an asterisk (*). Bibliographical citations are given with annotations at the end of the article. Then the set pieces are discussed and performance results are given.

Test sources	AMSR	Midi-Scan	Music-Reader	Note-Scan	OMR	SAM	Sight-Reader
Printed parts/band or orchestra	easy	somewhat easy	easy	tested	tested	being tested	tested
Printed parts/early music	—	—	—	—	—	—	tested
Printed lead sheets	—	easy	—	—	tested	—	tested
Printed scores/chamber music	somewhat easy	—	somewhat easy	tested	—	being tested	tested
Printed scores/orchestral	somewhat difficult	somewhat easy	somewhat easy	tested	—	being tested	tested
Printed scores/piano vocal (popular/folk)	easy	easy	somewhat difficult	tested	tested	easy	tested
Printed scores/choral	moderate	somewhat easy	somewhat easy	—	—	—	tested
Facsimiles/early printed music	—	—	—	—	—	—	—
Manuscripts/recent	difficult	somewhat easy	—	—	—	—	—
Manuscripts/early	—	—	difficult	—	—	—	—
Maximum number of parts in score	no maximum	16	9	no maximum	not relevant	not stated	not stated

Table 1. Repertories attempted in the testing of optical recognition software. Respondents were asked to indicate which ones had been attempted and to rate the results in achieving accurate recognition on a five-point scale ranging from easy to difficult. The *SightReader* response did not provide separate ratings but said that the relative difficulty depends on the musical content of the pages and the quality of the printing, a position that undoubtedly applies to the other programs as well.

Computing in Musicology

Feature	AMSR	Midi-Scan	Music-Reader	Note-Scan	OMR	SAM	Sight-Reader
Noteheads (black)	1	1	1	1	2	X	X
Noteheads (non-contiguous) in two-note chords	1	1	1	2	3	X	X
Noteheads (non-contiguous) in three-note chords	2	1	1	2	3	X	X
Stems	1	1	1	1	2	X	X
Stem directions	1	1	1	1	4	—	X
Clef signs	2	1	2	5	4	X	X
Time signatures	—	1	5	5	—	—	—
Key signatures	3	1	2	1	4	X	X
Accidentals	3	1	2	2	3	X	X
Gracenotes	—	—	3	—	—	—	—
Ornaments	—	—	3	—	—	—	—
Dynamics letters (*p, f*)	—	—	—	—	—	—	—
Articulation marks (staccato, etc.)	1	—	1	—	4	X	X
Tempo words	—	—	—	—	—	—	—
Text underlay	—	—	—	—	—	—	—
Crescendos, diminuendos	4	—	—	—	—	X	X
Beams	2	1	1	2	3	X	X
Braces	—	—	—	—	—	—	X
Brackets	—	—	—	—	—	—	X
Barlines (part)	1	1	1	2	2	X	X
Barlines (score)	2	1	1	2	—	X	X
Ties	2	1	3	X	—	—	X
Slurs	2	—	3	—	—	—	X
Tuplet numerals	—	—	—	—	—	—	—
Basso Continuo figuration	—	—	—	—	—	—	—
Guitar tablature	—	—	—	—	—	—	X

Table 2. Musical features supported by optical recognition software. Respondents were asked to score the competence of their programs in general in recognizing each feature on a sliding scale in which 1 = very easy to recognize and 5 = very difficult to recognize. Some respondents merely indicate which features are supported; these responses are represented by an X.

***Automatic Music Score Recogniser* (*AMSR*)**
Developers: Kia-Chuan Ng* and Roger D. Boyle
Location: The University of Leeds, England
Hardware/operating system: Unix (Silicon Graphics Indigo)
Scanning equipment: Hewlett Packard ScanJet Plus
Scanning resolution: 300 d.p.i.
Export format: Standard MIDI files
Intended applications: sound, printing, analysis
Anticipated date of availability: end of 1994

AMSR, which is being developed on a Unix workstation, is a graphics-to-sound translation program. It utilizes a screen display of the scanned bit-mapped image. There is no need to provide a screen display of the reconstructed score, since it does not aim to support a full range of music printing features. In consequence, however, there is currently no support for screen editing of the information. No information about the two sample pieces distributed was included in the response. However, the respondents report having tested their program on extracts from piano sonatas by Beethoven and Mozart and solo violin parts from Bach's sonatas and partitas.

The overall approach is described as one employing a method which directly reverses the process of music writing. Whereas a composer would normally write a notehead followed by a stem and/or a beam and lastly other markings such as slurs and ties, this group would first pick out long and thin features such as slurs and ties, followed by beams, then stems. In this way the complicated compound features are broken up into a lower graphical level of primitives before recognition.

Currently an effort is being made to use feedback from the *Recogniser* to control the segmentation into musical primitives automatically. Further information is available in the respondents' article on segmentation [see References].

Further information: Kia Chuan Ng, Division of Artificial Intelligence, School of Computer Studies, The University of Leeds, Leeds LS2 9JT, England, UK; tel.: +44 532/336798; fax: 532/335468; e-mail: *kia@scs.leeds.ac.uk*. Roger D. Boyle: *roger@scs.leeds.ac.uk*.

MidiScan
Respondent: Christopher Newell
Location: Musitek, Ojai, California
Hardware/operating system: MS-DOS/Windows 3.1 (286, 386, 486, PS II compatible)
Scanning equipment: any scanner capable of producing TIFF files can be used
Scanning resolution: 300 d.p.i.
Export format: Standard MIDI files, readable on the Mac, Atari, and Amiga as well as
   the originating DOS machine
Intended applications: sound via MIDI
Anticipated date of availability: available by direct mail from Musitek and through music
   merchants since May 1993

   MidiScan, the first commercial program for music recognition, is a self-contained system for converting printed information to Standard MIDI files. [It does not attempt to recognize objects not represented in a Standard MIDI file.] Major parts of the program have been written by Wladyslav Homenda (CPZH, Warsaw, Poland).

   Users need a hand-held or fullpage scanner to capture each page of the score as well as imaging software that is capable of auto-switching and outputs TIFF files. The TIFF files are loaded and processed sequentially by MIDISCAN. User intervention is required only for screen editing. The bit-mapped image which it displays can be edited on the screen with the Music Notation Object Recognition (MNOD) graphical editor.

   MidiScan quotes an approximate recognition time of 5 minutes per page of music.

Further information: Christopher Newell, Musitek Music Recognition Technologies, 410 Bryant Circle, Ste. K, Ojai, CA 93023-4209; tel.: (805) 646-8051; fax: (805) 646-8099; no e-mail address provided. [A review of *MidiScan* by Martin Roth appeared in the November 3 (1993) issue of Roth's electronic discussion of optical music recognition.]

MusicReader

Developers: William F. McGee* and Paul Merkley

Location: Ontario, Canada [originated at University of Ottawa]

Hardware/operating system: MS-DOS (386/16 MHrz)

Scanning equipment: Hewlett Packard ScanJet

Scanning resolution: 300 d.p.i.

Export formats: Standard MIDI, General MIDI, DARMS

Intended applications: sound, printing, analysis

Anticipated date of availability: January 1994 (beta-test version currently available)

MusicReader, on which an fuller description was separately submitted, provides display of a bit-mapped image. It produces both *DARMS* and MIDI files that can be read and edited using the *Note Processor*, a notation program for the PC. The reconstructed part or score can be displayed and edited using the *Note Processor*. *DARMS* data can also be used for analytical applications. *MusicReader*'s Standard and General MIDI files can also be used by MIDI notation programs and by MIDI hardware including synthesizers and tone generators. The MIDI files produced provide realizations for trills, mordents, turns, and arpeggios.

MusicReader software also offers an alternative input option to the user without a scanner, whereby a MIDI keyboard is used for pitch acquisition and a computer keyboard supplies duration. Output to both *DARMS* and MIDI is possible.

MusicReader has established a service bureau and offers scanning, with output in either format, at $5/page. Hardcopy is available at an additional $5/page.

Further information: William F. McGee, 73 Crystal Beach Drive, Nepean, Ontario, Canada K2H SN3; tel · 613/828-9130; fax: 828 9130; e-mail: *mcgee@citr.ee.mcglll.ca*. Paul Merkley, Department of Music, University of Ottawa, Ottawa, Canada K1N 6N5; tel.: (613) 564-9239; fax: (613) 564-5643; ; e-mail: *merkley@acadvml.uottawa.ca*. An extensive description of this system is provided in the Developer's Report on pp. 146-51.

NoteScan™

Respondent: Cindy Grande*

Location: Grande Software, Inc., Seattle, WA

Hardware/operating system: Macintosh IIci (25MHz); conversion to MS-DOS

Scanning equipment: Apple One Scanner

Scanning resolution: 200 and 300 d.p.i.

Export format: NoteScan

Intended applications: printing, sound, analysis

Anticipated date of availability: demo disk available; to be offered as enhancements to two notation programs—*Nightingale* and *Music Printer Plus*—by Temporal Acuity Products in Spring 1994

NoteScan converts recognized information to an intermediate file format (*NoteScan* NTIF), from which it may be converted to a wide variety of proprietary formats used by commercial notation programs. Any scanner producing TIFF files may be used. Existing commercial agreements for its use are non-exclusive.

The Macintosh version produces bitmapped images on the screen. These may be edited using programs such as Adobe *Photoshop*. The reconstructed score may be displayed, enlarged, reduced, and edited in music applications programs such as *Music Printer Plus* and *Nightingale*.

Cindy Grande is the developer of the recognizer logic. Charles Rose wrote the *Nightingale* interface. Gary Barber wrote the MS-DOS adaptation and the interface to *Music Printer Plus*.

Further information: Cindy Grande, President, Grande Software, Inc., 19004 37th Avenue South, Seattle, WA 98188; tel.: (206) 439-9828; fax: (206) 824-2612. Temporal Acuity Products, Inc., is located as 300 120th Avenue N.E., Bldg. 1, Bellevue, WA 98005; tel.: (800) 426-2673. NoteScan is a trademark of Grande Software, Inc.

Optical Music Recognition (*OMR*)
Respondent: Martin Roth
Location: Eidgenössische Technische Hochschule, Zurich, Switzerland
Hardware/operating system: Unix (Sun, NeXT)
Scanning equipment: various
Scanning resolution: 200 and 300 d.p.i.
Export format: *Lipsia*
Intended applications: printing
Anticipated date of availability: undertaken as thesis project; future plans pending

Development of the *OMR* program was initiated as a thesis project in engineering and computer science (1993) and is not directly comparable with other programs listed here. It is intended to support automatic recognition of music fonts. The program, in *C*, concentrates on such features as a bounding box and estimates of weight and center of gravity. It does not attempt to supply semantic information needed for interpretation of captured symbols. It has been designed to work with *Lipsia*, a notation editor developed several years ago at ETH by Giovanni Müller [see *CM 1987*, Illustration #44, p. 71].

OMR is oriented toward object acquisition. Bit-mapped images may be edited using the workstation utilities *X-loadimage* and *X-view*. A semantic lexicon is used to determine placement by *Lipsia*; *OMR* has no semantic constraints. A reconstructed score may be shown using Display postscript on a NeXT workstation. Development of *Lipsia* has now ceased, and the future path of *OMR*'s development is uncertain. The program is unusual in handling an arbitrary number of staves.

Further Information: Martin Roth, ETH Zurich, IPS - RZ F16, Steinstrasse 58, CH-8003 Zurich, Switzerland; tel.: +10 1/256 55 68; 1/463 13 61; fax: 1/261 04 68; e-mail: *roth@ips.id.ethz.ch*. Roth moderates an electronic discussion of optical music recognition (*omr@ips.ed.ethz.ch*) and maintains an electronic bibliography in several formats (details given on p. 145).

Score Analyzing Maestro (SAM)
Developers: Elizabeth C. Botha* and students (Karl Geggus, Johan Boot)
Location: University of Pretoria, South Africa
Hardware/operating system: MS-DOS (486/33)
Scanning equipment: Hewlett Packard ScanJet
Scanning resolution: 300 d.p.i.
Export format: MOD (Amiga) format [supported by Soundblaster card]
Intended applications: sound, conventional music notation, Braille music notation,
 analysis, educational software
Anticipated date of availability: first half of 1994

    SAM is a self-contained acquisition program for the PC oriented entirely toward sound output. It does not provide for screen display and editing of the reconstructed score. Pitch and duration are captured and plans are underway to implement volume level and change parameters in output files from the recognition of dynamics indicators in scanned scores. Support for Standard MIDI files and General MIDI is planned.

    The developers intend to make the program available electronically by FTP. For current information via the Internet send the command:

At mainframe prompt:	**ftp *ftp.ee.up.ac.za***
Logon:	**anonymous**
To change directories:	**cd */u/ftp/pub/musiek***
To prepare for a binary transfer:	**binary**

Retrieve (**get**) the file *readme.tex*. The documentation files are updated as changes in the program are implemented.

Further information: Dr. Elizabeth C. Botha, Dept. of Electrical and Electronic Engineering, University of Pretoria, Pretoria 000 2, South Africa; tel.: +27 12/420-2981; fax: 12/437837; e-mail: *botha@ford.ee.up.ac.za*.

SightReader

Respondent: Nicholas P. Carter

Location: University of Surrey, Guildford, England

Hardware/operating system: Unix (Sun, Hewlett Packard, NeXT) for development; MS-DOS (486) for output

Scanning equipment: Hewlett Packard ScanJet (or other scanner producing TIFF files)

Scanning resolution: 300 d.p.i.

Export format: *SCORE* input files and *SightReader* files

Intended applications: sound, notation, analysis, electronic distribution

Anticipated date of availability: undetermined; licensed to Coda Music Technology

SightReader has been developed on Unix workstations and makes use of separate utilities, for example to provide a scrollable screen view of bit-mapped images converted to TIFF files. The bitmap can be cropped and scaled. The image can be reduced or enlarged. *SightReader* exports files to the input format used by *SCORE*, a notation program for the PC. Parts of *SightReader* are now running on a PC.

In separate experiments, *SightReader* was used to explore the capture of information from late Renaissance part books containing white mensural notation [see "Segmentation" in the Bibliography] and with the reconstruction of an early twentieth-century score [see "Walton"].

Further information: Dr. Nicholas P. Carter, Department of Physics, University of Surrey, Guildford, Surrey GU2 5XH, England, UK; tel.: +44 483/300800; fax: 483/300803; e-mail: *N.Carter@ph.surrey.ac.uk*. Also see the Developer's Report on pp. 152-58.

Set Pieces

In the interests of creating a common focus for discussion, two musical examples were distributed with the questionnaire. The first was a violin part from Handel's opera *Radamisto*.

Example 1. Excerpt from Handel's *Radamisto*.

This example contains beamed eighth, sixteenth, and thirty-second notes, as well as single quarter and eighth notes with a key signature involving four sharps and numerous accidentals of various kinds. It also has half, quarter, and eighth rests. In addition it includes a tempo indication, dynamics markings, a multibar abbreviation, a measure number, and a trill sign. This example was based on a recent print generated by computer at CCARH.

Example 2. Excerpt from a Clementi sonatina in G Major.

The second example was an eight-bar excerpt from a well known piano sonatina by Clementi. It contains half, quarter, eighth, and sixteenth notes (some with dots and/or beams), quarter rests, and repeat signs. It is mainly different from the first example in that (a) it is in a two-stave score, (b) it contains numerous slurs, and (3) it contains fingering numbers over many notes. This example was published in the early twentieth century by conventional means.

Respondents were given the option of scanning either or both of these examples or an item of their own choice. They were asked to record the time required to go, in four steps, from the original material to its complete, accurate reconstruction. Machine speeds were not uniformly reported. Respondents were asked to compute a statistical result representing the accuracy of the automatically captured data. In the absence of a commonly accepted way of making such a computation, they were also asked to explain their own means and to suggest a way of providing a uniform measure of competence.

Test Reports and Results

Respondents' reports provide little basis for comparison not only because of differences in hardware, operating systems, and software environments but also because some respondents did not provide precise numbers or scanned material other than what was sent. One group, *AMSR*, did not provide scanning times for this survey.

MidiScan

MidiScan [see description on p. 122] reported the following scanning times for the Handel example:

Operation	Handel
Input time	0:12
Image processing time	0:20
Screen correction time	0:30
Output time	0:20
Total elapsed time	1:22

Table 3. *MidiScan*: Scanning, processing, and output time in minutes and seconds. Output was to MIDI files. Processing was done on a 486.

Note that since a MIDI file is the objective, this scan could exclude the dynamics marks, trill signs, and tempo words ("Andante larghetto") and that no printed notation is produced by *MidiScan*.

MusicReader

MusicReader's tests (Table 4) were run on a 386/16 MHz PC.

Operation	Handel	Clementi
Input time	0:16	0:22
Image processing time	4:16	8:50
Screen correction time	3:05	6:28
Output time	0:38	0:30
Total elapsed time	8:15	16:10

Table 4. *MusicReader*: scanning time in minutes and seconds. "Screen correction" represents time spent editing *DARMS* code. Output time represents *DARMS*-to-MIDI conversion and audio playback. Processing was done on a 386.

Since other DOS contributors offered results based on 486 performance, we asked *MusicReader* for an estimate of times that would be achieved if the tests had been performed on a 486. These were roughly calculated to be one third of the values shown in Table 4. However, it would not necessarily follow that screen correction time, the most substantial part of the process, would fall by this much, since it is dependent largely on manual skills.

```
I1 !G !K4# !MC,OO@Andante larghetto$ 5RE ((8S.D,VF (9TD))) /
I1 (30ED (9S.D (8TD))) (32ED (31S.D (30TD)))
   (33ED (31S.D (30TD))) (9ED (30S.D (31TD))) /
I1 30QD 5RE ((9S.D (8TD))) (7ED 6ED) 5RE ((31S.D (30TD))) /
I1 (9##ED 30ED) 4RE ((30S.D (9*#TD))) (8#ED 9ED 7ED 8*ED) /
I1 !G !K4# 6ED 4QU ((3SU 2SU)) (3EU (2SU 1SU)) (OE.U,OT (1SU)) /
I1 1QU 5RQ 5RH /
I1 R4W /
I1 5RH 5RQ 5RE ((7S.D,VP (6TD))) /
I1 (5#ED 6ED) 5RE ((6S.D (5*TD))) (4#EU 5EU) 5RQ /
I1 5RH 4RE 7ED 8QD /
```

Example 3. *DARMS* code for the Handel example produced by *MusicReader*.

Since *MusicReader* supports both a print code (*DARMS*; cf. Example 3) and a sound code (MIDI), it must support a broader range of objects than if it supported only one output format. Therefore in the screen editing phase for the Handel example *MusicReader* would be obliged to add codes for dynamics and tempo words; in the Clementi example the dynamics and fingering numbers would need to be added. The commentary on *MusicReader* is on p. 123. A substantial description is given independently on pp. 146-51.

NoteScan

NoteScan, unknown to us when our survey was distributed, was located shortly before we went to press. In lieu of the distributed examples, its respondent provided results of other timed tests; accuracy rates above 90% were claimed. These tests were all run on a Macintosh IIci/25MHz with output to both the *NoteScan* file format and to *Nightingale*. Times reported below (in minutes and seconds) do not include editing:

1. Bach: Two-Part Invention in G Minor, BWV 782, Bars 1-10,
scanned from a typeset original of excellent quality at 200 d.p.i.   3:30

2. Beethoven: Piano Sonata Op. 81a ("Les Adieux"), First Movement, Bars 146-175,
scanned from a typeset original of excellent quality at 200 d.p.i.   4:10

3. Haydn: (unidentified) String Quartet in F, final 15 bars of a fast movement,
scanned from a miniature score at 300 d.p.i.   5:20

4. "Feeling Good" [piano/vocal with guitar chords], Bars 1-10 [excluding text and
guitar chords]; scanned from a computer-set arrangement [*Finale*] at 300 d.p.i.   3:10

5. Leo Ornstein: Piano Sonata No. 9, 20-bar excerpt with complex voicing,
numerous accidentals, *etc.*; scanned from typeset original at 300 d.p.i.   7:30

Examples 4a, b, and c show a three-bar passage from this excerpt:

© 1990 Leo Ornstein. Used by permission of
Poon Hill Press, Woodside, CA 94062

Example 4a. Leo Ornstein: Piano Sonata No. 8—original print.

Example 4b. Leo Ornstein: Piano Sonata No. 8—unedited *NoteScan* results.

Example 4c. Leo Ornstein: Piano Sonata No. 8—*NoteScan* results edited and transposed using *Nightingale*.

OMR

OMR reported scanning time only, with the following results:

| Handel | 0:22 |
| Clementi | 1:03 |

In lieu of other measures of time, the respondent for *OMR* provided actual output from his program (shown below). His comments point to the kinds of problems that those who experiment with optical recognition often encounter. He remarked that (1) the examples were "very light"; (2) the noteheads were smaller than those on which his program had been trained; and (3) when noteheads are not recognized, stems can be mistaken for barlines.

Example 5a. *OMR*: Unedited scan of the Handel example.

Example 5b. *OMR*: Unedited scan of the Clementi example.

Examples 5a and b illustrate one feature that occurs commonly in optical recognition: mistaken object types. In Example 5a dynamics indications have been replaced by white noteheads. In Example 5b it appears that the fingering numeral 2 has been read as the accent > and the numeral 3 as the accent < . Although in this case the error is obvious, in other situations, errors generated by scanners can be hard to detect visually and may survive until the data is actually put to use in an application. Recognition software can also generate completely spurious objects, especially from specks of dirt on the scanned page. Thus the proofreading of scanned material is often more cumbersome than that of ordinary typesetting.

SAM

The developers of *SAM* provided scanning times for both the Clementi example and a Bach keyboard minuet. Times for the Clementi example are shown in Table 5.

Operation	Clementi
Input time	5:15
Image processing time	6:10
Screen correction time	5:55
Output time	2:20
Total elapsed time	19: 40

Table 5. *SAM*: Time (in minutes and seconds) elapsed in the scan of the 8-bar Clementi example. A 486/33 was used.

Example 6. *SAM*: Final staff of the Bach minuet scanned.

```
Unit 20                                    Unit 21
Line0 xs 0 ys 121 xe 264 ye 117            Line0 xs 0 ys 122 xe 232 ye 119
Line1 xs 0 ys 142 xe 264 ye 138            Line1 xs 0 ys 142 xe 232 ye 140
Line2 xs 0 ys 163 xe 264 ye 159            Line2 xs 0 ys 163 xe 232 ye 161
Line3 xs 0 ys 184 xe 264 ye 180            Line3 xs 0 ys 184 xe 232 ye 182
Line4 xs 0 ys 205 xe 264 ye 201            Line4 xs 0 ys 205 xe 232 ye 203
Line5 xs 0 ys 331 xe 264 ye 326            Line5 xs 0 ys 330 xe 232 ye 327
Line6 xs 0 ys 352 xe 264 ye 348            Line6 xs 0 ys 351 xe 232 ye 348
Line7 xs 0 ys 372 xe 264 ye 368            Line7 xs 0 ys 372 xe 232 ye 369
Line8 xs 0 ys 393 xe 264 ye 389            Line8 xs 0 ys 393 xe 232 ye 390
Line9 xs 0 ys 414 xe 264 ye 410            Line9 xs 0 ys 414 xe 232 ye 410
Crotchet1 xp 135 yp 183 xs 0 ys 0          Minim xp 43 yp 184 xs 0 ys 0
Crotchet1 xp 215 yp 191 xs 0 ys 0          Minim xp 43 yp 215 xs 0 ys 0
Crotchet2 xp 40 yp 163 xs 0 ys 0           Minim xp 43 yp 240 xs 0 ys 0
Crotchet2 xp 86 yp 143 xs 0 ys 0           Crotchet1 xp 38 yp 341 xs 0 ys 0
Crotchet1 xp 134 yp 392 xs 0 ys 0          Crotchet1 xp 177 yp 411 xs 0 ys 0
Crotchet1 xp 39 yp 341 xs 0 ys 0           Crotchet1 xp 106 yp 372 xs 0 ys 0
Crotchet1 xp 211 yp 370 xs 0 ys 0          Dotdurmod xp 71 yp 169 xs 16 ys 8
Staccato xp 134 yp 218 xs 8 ys 7           Dotdurmod xp 72 yp 213 xs 16 ys 9
Staccato xp 214 yp 219 xs 8 ys 6           Dotdurmod xp 71 yp 239 xs 16 ys 8
Decrescendo xp 31 yp 240 xs 216 ys 30      Staccato xp 41 yp 312 xs 8 ys 6
Staccato xp 212 yp 336 xs 8 ys 6           Staccato xp 109 yp 335 xs 8 ys 6
Staccato xp 132 yp 424 xs 0 ys 0           Staccato xp 173 yp 439 xs 8 ys 5
```

Example 7. *SAM*: File excerpt representing the last two bars of Example 6.

The minuet is one of 32 bars—four times the length of the Clementi example. It is also somewhat more difficult (at least in the second half) in texture as well as number and proximity of symbols than the Clementi example. These factors should be taken into account in examining the performance figures given in Table 6.

Operation	Bach minuet
Input time	4:40
Image processing time	21:47
Screen correction time	4:30
Output time	1:13
Total elapsed time	32:10

Table 6. *SAM*: Time required to recognize a 32-bar Bach minuet.

SightReader

SightReader submitted information concerning the scanning of one page of a Haydn symphony. The original is shown as Example 8. This has more staves (9) per system than the other examples submitted but is relatively free of objects other than black notes, accidentals, beams, and slurs.

Example 8. *SightReader*: One system from Haydn's Symphony No. 8 (original image, reduced).

This example provides a useful opportunity to address the issue of counting the number of graphic objects, which may be significantly greater than the number of musical objects as we normally conceive of them. Horizontal line objects, for example, may be said to include 1 system, or 9 staves, or 45 staff lines. Vertical line objects include 8 barlines (each presented as two graphic objects, because of the section breaks) as well as the barline that forms part of the brace. A graphics recogniser must take separate account of the curved end pieces and the two curly brackets. This example contains 256 noteheads; these are attached to 254 stems. Ten stems have flags. Musicians would be inclined to consider these 520 graphics objects to make up 256 musical entities ("the notes"). We also find 24 eighth rests and 7 whole rests. There are 20 single beams (of three eighth notes) and 30 double beams (of six sixteenth notes); there are also 30 slurs. By way of miscellaneous markings, the example contains 9 clef signs, 36 accidentals, 9 dots of prolongation, 9 dynamics signs, and 1 rehearsal number (containing two graphic parts—a box and a numeral).

SightReader provided samples of acquisition before and after correction. These are shown as Examples 9 (below) and 10 (on the following page).

Example 9. *SightReader*: Lower system of Haydn symphony after acquisition and translation to *SCORE* but before correction. Error categories are coded A (superfluous notes), B (erroneous pitch), and C (error in use of accidental).

Notice that in Example 9 there are superfluous notes (Error Type A; 4 instances), mistaken pitches (Type B; 2 instances), and superfluous, misconstrued, and misplaced accidentals (Type C; 8 instances). These errors were attributed to *SCORE*'s difficulty in placing barlines accurately. Slurs and beams are captured by *SightReader*, while dynamics markings are added editorially in *SCORE* files (Example 10). Durational values with the wrong visual grammar (*i.e.*, quarter rests in place of two eighths; 11 instances) are also corrected editorially.

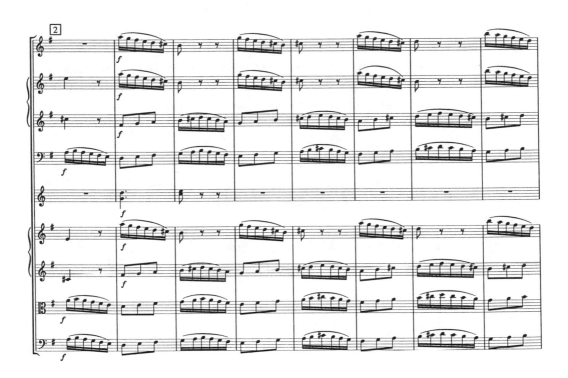

Example 10. *SightReader*: Same system after editorial correction using *SCORE*.

Operation	Haydn symphony excerpt
Input time	00:30
Image processing time	00:48
Screen correction time	19:30
Output time	01:15
Total elapsed time	22:08

Table 7. *SightReader*: Elapsed time (in minutes and seconds) in the recognition of one page (two systems including the one shown above) of Haydn's Symphony No. 8.

Quantifying Program Performance

The easiest way to rate the efficiency of the system is to count the number of objects on the page and express the number recognized correctly as a percentage. It is not necessarily a very satisfactory method, since the misrecognition of one object can obviate the correct recognition of another that is contingent. From the user's point of view, some objects may be worth weighting more heavily than others, but such weightings would be relative to the repertory at hand.

We asked respondents to indicate the relative reliability of their programs in correctly recognizing all the object types that occur in the two examples we distributed. Their self-assessments are shown in Table 8.

Object	Midi-Scan	Music-Reader	Note-Scan	OMR	SAM
white notes	x	5	5	4	2
black notes	1	1	1	2	2
rests	2	2	3	3	2
stems	1	1	1	2	2
beams	2	1	2	3	3
clefs	1	3	5	4	2
barlines	1	1	2	2	1
braces	x	x	x	x	x
sharp signs	1	1	2	2	2
natural signs	1	1	2	2	2
fermatas	x	x	x	x	x
slurs	x	4	x	x	x

Table 8. Self-estimates of levels of accuracy in recognition of objects. An x means the object is not attempted. A score of 1 means it is easily captured. *SightReader* did not provide evaluations.

Measures of the rapidity with which a musical passage can be interpreted give only a very preliminary indication of software performance. Accuracy is essential if optical recognition is to become a useful tool.

How might accuracy be assessed? We asked our respondents to suggest ways in which this might be computed. The predominant view expressed was that one might divide the total number of objects correctly identified by the total number of objects in the example. If, for example, there are 100 objects in an example and 60 are correctly identified, a score of 60% would be achieved.

In moving from the generalization to the actuality, a number of considerations arise:

• In all cases mentioned here there is a discrepancy between the number of objects present and the number attempted. This is a result of the implementation of object classes one by one (Table 8 indicates classes unattempted with an "x"), since at the present time there is no program that attempts to identify all the object classes present in the relatively simple examples that we circulated. The program is seen to be more competent if the total number of objects correctly identified is divided by the total number attempted.

Suppose that there are 100 objects in an example, 80 fall into classes that are attempted, and 60 are correctly identified. Whereas by Method 1 (total present/total identified) a score of 60% would be attained, by Method 2 (total attempted/total identified) a score of 75% would be attained. To the end user who is interested in a competent end result, the first measure gives a fairer picture.

• Systems do not all define objects in the same way. A "note" may be an indivisible unit in one system whereas in another a notehead and a notestem may be classed as two separate objects. Two evaluators scanning the same hypothetical example may find 100 objects if the composite note is considered to be the smallest unit of information and 125 objects if the graphical parts of the note (heads, stems, flags, *et al.*) are taken to be individual objects.

• Grande suggests also tabulating spurious objects falsely recognized and subtracting them from the total correctly identified before dividing by the total present.

The first consideration is compounded by the substitution of "friendly examples," that is, those lacking object classes that the program does not attempt to recognize, since there will be little discrepancy between the first and second methods of calculation. *SightReader*, for example, claims an accuracy of 94.2% in the Haydn example presented. This is based on 778 *SCORE* items in the file on which the reconstruction is based. Among these 45 required correction. The page in question contained the system shown in Example 8 and the preceding system, which is very comparable in musical detail. It is clear that by defining objects in a graphical sense rather than a musical sense the numbers of items is elastic and could have been greater still [see pp. 135-6].

Another issue that complicates measures of performance is how the same items would be treated if encoded (*e.g.*, alphanumerically) as input to the program used to edit the example. While no system in common use requires separate representation of every staff line and many facilitate the creation of a template to set up systems, there is some open-endedness in most systems. The *DARMS*-based *Note Processor* would create the rehearsal number, for example, by assembling two right angles to form a box and placing a numeral within it (3 objects); *SCORE* in some instances requires insetting a second beam to create sixteenth-note groups from eighth-note groups. In notation programs there has always been a tradeoff between ease of use and degree of control over the result. In evaluating software for optical recognition it will be as important as ever to remember that intended use is the most important factor to consider in selecting a system.

Those whose sole objective is to acquire files (*e.g.*, MIDI) for sound applications can happily ignore the handling of beams and rehearsal numbers as well as system layout and the like. Reengineering of systems designed in the first instance for sound output to support complex notational output remains a difficult task.

Considering that the field of optical recognition is still in its infancy, it would be inappropriate to insist on common examples, since it is in the nature of scanning programs to perform best on material that resembles the material used for training. This will inevitably vary widely from program to program. As we demonstrated at the beginning, the graphic quality of materials is generally poorer than one would assume on a cursory glance, but there are many different kinds of typographical poverty. At a technical level, no two kinds may correspond in the problems they pose. Thus, good editing tools for passing the scanned result to an applications program become essential. The route to competent programs for sound output should be shorter than that to programs for notation, since less information needs to be conveyed.

The Future

Two Japanese researchers with substantial experience in the development of optical recognition, Hirokazu Kato and Seiji Inokuchi, assert that the goal of finding a single method for recognizing all musical symbols may be unrealistic. Their work uses a five-layer processing model that ascends from the pixel level through "primitives" (symbol elements such as flags and beams), complete symbols, and musical meaning (pitch and duration) to interpretations of the acquired information. This model implicitly suggests the degree to which the intellectual obstacles to accurate recognition arise from the complexity of the visual grammar of music.

An Annotated Bibliography
including Theses-in-Progress

Baumann, Stefan. "*DOREMIDI*: Document Recognition of Printed Scores and Transformation into MIDI." Master's thesis, German Research Center for Artificial Intelligence, 1992.

> Available as a printed research report from the above Center, P.O. Box 2080, 67608 Kaiserslautern, Germany. Further information: Stefan Baumann, German Research Center for AI, Erwin-Schroedingerstr., 67663 Kaiserslautern, Germany; tel.: +49 631/205-3343; fax: 631/205-3210; e-mail: *baumann@dfki.uni-kl.de.*

Bainbridge, David. "Preliminary Experiments in Musical Score Recognition." Undergraduate project, Dept. of Computer Science, University of Edinburgh, 1991.

> This author's work continues, with output to *CSound*, at the Dept. of Computing, University of Canterbury, Christchurch, New Zealand; e-mail: *dbain @cosc.canterbury.ac.nz.*

Baumann, Stefan. "Transforming Printed Piano Music into MIDI" in the *Proceedings of the Workshop on Syntactical and Structural Pattern Recognition, Sep.1992* (Bern).

Blostein, Dorothea, and Henry S. Baird. "A Critical Survey of Music Image Analysis" in *Structured Document Image Analysis*, ed. Henry S. Baird, Horst Bunke, and Kazuhiko Yamamoto (Berlin: Springer-Verlag, 1992), pp. 405-34.

> Review of terminology, procedures (line adjacency graph, run-length histograms, template matching), symbol classification methods, and a useful list of references.

Blostein, Dorothea, and Nicholas P. Carter. "Recognition of Music Notation: SSPR '90 Working Group Report" in *Structured Document Image Analysis*, ed. Henry S. Baird, Horst Bunke, and Kazuhiko Yamamoto (Berlin: Springer-Verlag, 1992), pp. 373-4.

> Report of a workshop on Syntactic and Structural Pattern Recognition held at Murray Hill, NJ on 13-15 June 1990.

Carter, Nicholas P., and Richard A. Bacon. "Automatic Recognition of Printed Music" in *Structured Document Image Analysis*, ed. Henry S. Baird, Horst Bunke, and Kazuhiko Yamamoto (Berlin: Springer-Verlag, 1992), pp. 456-65.

> Reports progress in developing an object recognition system which is independent of font types and sizes, with scanned examples of keyboard passages from C. P. E. Bach [as shown in *CM 1991*] translated into *SCORE* code.

Carter, Nicholas P. "A New Edition of Walton's *Façade* Using Automatic Score Recognition" in *Advances in Structural and Syntactic Pattern Recognition*, ed. Horst Bunke (Singapore: World Scientific), pp. 352-62.

Describes problems encountered in replicating a printed score from the early twentieth century.

Carter, Nicholas P. "Segmentation and Preliminary Recognition of Madrigals Notated in White Mensural Notation," *Machine Vision and Applications* 5 (1992), 223-30.

Describes efforts to recognize printed notation used in the late sixteenth and early seventeenth centuries.

Choi, James. "Optical Recognition of the Printed Musical Score." M.S. thesis, Northwestern University, [1992]. Further information: *phantom@merle.acns.nwu.edu*.

Clarke, Alastair, Malcolm Brown, and Mike Thorne. "Problems to be faced by the Developers of Computer Based Automatic Music Recognisers," *Proceedings of the International Computer Music Conference 1990* (San Francisco: Computer Music Association, 1990), pp. 345-347.

Couasnon, Bertrand. "Segmentation et reconnaissance de partitions musicales guidées par une grammaire."

Couasnon's grammatical approach to recognition of printed scores involves a dual neural net/rule-base system approach to recognition of printed scores. Further information: IRISA, INSA - Dept. Informatique, 20, av. des Buttes de Coesmes, 35043 Rennes Cedex, France; tel.: +33 99/28-64-91; fax: 99/63-67-05; e-mail: *couasnon@irisa.fr*.

Fujinaga, Ichiro. "Optical Music Recognition using Projections." M.A. thesis, McGill University, 1988.

This project has been continued in doctoral research about OMR software scheduled for completion in 1994. Further information: Ichiro Fujinaga, Peabody Conservatory of Music, 1 E. Mt. Vernon Place, Baltimore MD, 21202; e-mail: *ich@music.mcgill.ca*.

Fujinaga, Ichiro, Bo Alphonce, and Bruce Pennycook. "Issues in the Design of an Optical Music Recognition System," *Proceedings of the International Computer Music Conference 1989* (San Francisco: CMA, 1989), pp. 113-6.

Fujinaga, Ichiro, Bo Alphonce, Bruce Pennycook and Natalie Boisvert. "Optical Recognition of Musical Notation by Computer," *Computers in Music Research* 1 (1989), 161-4.

Fujinaga, Ichiro, Bo Alphonce, Bruce Pennycook, and Glendon Diener. "Interactive Optical Music Recognition," *Proceedings of the International Computer Music Conference 1992* (San Jose: 1992), pp. 117-21.

This system developed at McGill University in Montreal runs on the NeXT workstation and outputs files to the public-domain *Nutation* editor developed by Diener. The program builds a database of previously identified symbols. Success is reported with both printed and manuscript sources.

Itagaki, Takabumi, Masayuki Isogai, Shuji Hashimoto, and Sadamu Ohteru. "Automatic Recognition of Several Types of Musical Notation" in *Structured Document Image Analysis*, ed. Henry S. Baird, Horst Bunke, and Kazuhiko Yamamoto (Berlin: Springer-Verlag, 1992), pp. 466-76.

Describes the use of *SMX [Standard Musical Expression]* as an intermediate output format for scanned notation to be routed to diverse end-uses including printing scores, Braille scores, and electronic performance. The test repertory consisted of piano works including a Chopin étude and the Fantaisie-impromptu. Experiments with Braille input and recognition of Labanotation were also conducted.

Kato, Hirokazu, and Seiji Inokuchi. "A Recognition System for Printed Piano Music using Musical Knowledge and Constraints" in *Structured Document Image Analysis*, ed. Henry S. Baird, Horst Bunke, and Kazuhiko Yamamoto (Berlin: Springer-Verlag, 1992), pp. 435-55.

The authors describe their five-tiered approach to recognition and offer accuracy figures for four piano works scanned ranging from 83% (the second movement of Beethoven's Sonata "Pathétique") to 96% (Beethoven's "Für Elise").

Leplumey, Ivan, and Jean Camillerapp. "Comparison of Region Labelling [in the] Musical Score," *Proceedings of the First International Conference on Document Analysis* (St. Malo, 1991), pp. 674-82. Also in French in *AFRCET: 8ᵉ Congrès Reconnaissance des Formes et Intelligence Artificielle* (Lyon: Villeurbanne, 1991), 3, 1045-1052.

Concentrates on segmentation algorithms to facilitate score recognition.

Leroy, Annick, and Bertrand Couasnon. "Editeur plume multifonction: application a un editeur plume musical" ("Multipurpose Pen Editor: Application to a Pen-based Music Editor").

A pen-based music editor is under development in this thesis-in-progress. Further information: Poste 4204 IRISA, INSA - Dept. Informatique. 35043 Rennes Cedex, France; tel.: +33 99/28-64-00; e-mail: *couasnon@irisa.fr*.

Ng, Kia-Chuan, and Roger D. Boyle. "Segmentation of Music Primitives," *Proceedings of the British Machine Vision Conference 1992*, pp. 472-80.

A fuller explanation of the approach described herein.

Pennycook, Bruce, "Towards Advanced Optical Music Recognition," *Advanced Imaging* (April, 1990).

Perrotti, F. A., and R. A. Lotufo. "Pré-processamento, Extração de Atributos e Primeiro Nível de Classificação para un Sistema de Reconhecimento Ótico de Símbolos Musicais" ["Preprocessing, Feature Extraction, and First Classification Level for an Optical Recognition System"] in *VI Brazilian Symposium in Computer Graphics and Image Processing, SIBGRAPI. 19-22 October 1993*. Recife (Brazil), 1993.

A solution for the preprocessing, feature extraction, and first level of classification in optical music recognition is presented. The attributes are extracted from a thinned and vectorized image of the score. Critical points and their supporting environs are matched and clustered to identify candidate symbols. Experimental results are supported.

Further information: *perrotti@dca.fee.unicamp.br* and *lotufo@dca.fee.unicamp.br*.

Prerau, David. "Computer Pattern Recognition of Standard Engraved Music Notation." Ph.D. dissertation, Massachusetts Institute of Technology, 1970.

Although the amount of music the author was able to scan was extremely limited, the thought he applied to the task has remained fundamental in most projects originating in recent years.

Roth, Martin. "Optical Music Recognition Bibliography." Electronic text. Zurich: ETH, December 1992.

A recent compilation incorporating references from earlier bibliographies by Alastair Clarke, Henry Baird, Dorothea Blostein, and Karl Tombre. Readers are welcome to supply additions by sending them to *roth@ips.id.ethz.ch*. The material is available by FTP to *maggia.ethz.ch* (129.132.17.1), login *ftp*, directory */pub/roth/omrbib*.

Sonka, Milan, Vaclav Hlavac, and Roger Boyle. *Image Processing, Analysis, and Machine Vision*. London: Chapman and Hall, 1993.

See the contribution on *AMSR*.

Wolman, Amnon, James Choi, Shahab Asgharzadeh, and Jason Kahana.   "Recognition of Handwritten Music Notation," *Proceedings of the International Computer Music Conference 1992* (San Jose: 1992), pp. 125-7.

Describes research based on the premise that while a program which reads handwritten music could probably read printed music, the reverse is not true. Users are required to write music on commercially available printed score paper.

Yadid, Orly, Eliyahu Brutman, Lior Dvir, Moti Gerner, and Uri Shimony.   "*RAMIT*: [A] Neural Network for Recognition of Musical Notes," *Proceedings of the International Computer Music Conference 1992* (San Jose: 1992), pp. 128-31.

Describes the Neocognitron, a neural network model for visual recognition of black and white patterns.

Note: An extensive bibliography of writings on optical recognition is maintained by Martin Roth. It is accessible by FTP to *maggia.ethz.ch* [129.132.17.1] in the directory */pub/roth/omrbib*. Both compressed and uncompressed files are available.

MusicReader:
An Interactive Optical Music Recognition System

The *MusicReader* is an interactive one-pass optical music recognition system. It can capture information from a printed score and translate it to both a *DARMS* file (for printing) and a MIDI file (for playback) in a reasonable time. The system, which is implemented on a 640k 386/486 personal computer, supports interactive software requiring the use of a mouse, computer keyboard, and color display. We have adopted the basic approach developed by David Prerau for his dissertation at the Massachusetts Institute of Technology in 1970. This approach follows scanning with the removal of staff lines, the identification of connected pixel components, the classification of resulting musical entities, and the production of *DARMS* code as output.

The heart of our system is the one-pass classifier, which includes a robust staffline remover, and an integrated beam and chord analyzer. In its current state of development, our technology can facilitate computer-aided analysis, reorchestration, and (re)printing. *MusicReader*'s performance is best on monophonic sources in standard music notation (such as fake books and part scores), moderate on simpler piano scores, and fair on more complex music.

The review of the field made recently by Dorothea Blostein and Henry Baird makes it unnecessary to discuss previous work. In our view an understanding of the work of Prerau and Nicholas Carter, whose work began in the late Eighties at the University of Surrey, England, is essential to progress in this field.

The Music Reader System

The following five sets of computer data, discussed below, are used:

      1. A pixel representation of the musical score
      2. A file containing the classified connected components
with horizontal and vertical placement
      3. A *DARMS* representation
      4. A Brinkman score representation
      5. A Standard MIDI file

Interactive routines are used in the scanning process (to generate the pixel representation), in the classification process, and, normally, in the editing of the *DARMS* text file. Each routine is described in detail below.

We have found that with present computer technology, the best results are obtained through the analysis of connected staves representing several measures. Backtracking is not used in the classifier; this results in advantages and some minor disadvantages.

1. Scanner Program

A considerable portion of time is spent in the output of the scanning and input of the classification process: the files are large. A 2-inch segment of an 8-1/2 by 11-inch page takes 2 x 300 x 8.5 x 300 pixels, *i.e.*, 1.6 megapixels. Data compression techniques such as those used for facsimile transmission can reduce the size considerably, but these require coding and decoding. Since the pixels are thrown away anyway, we have opted for an intermediate position and use run encoding of the black pixels. The use of 16-bit integers is all that is required. Typical file lengths are 100 to 200 kilobytes. Therefore we have a file consisting, for each scanned line, of the beginning and end of each run of black pixels. An end-of-line marker (-1) is used to indicate the end of a line.

For staff-line identification purposes, the image must be a rotated one, as if the scanning had gone from left to right, rather than from top to bottom. This can be done in two ways: turning the page around, or doing a software rotation. The difficulty with a software rotation is that it requires a large memory for the required pointer arithmetic, limiting the number of staffs that may be readily scanned to five or so.

In the course of the project, we have developed utilities that will translate TIFF files and unrotated run-encoded files. A utility to remove short white runs is sometimes of use. For the scanning process itself, a series of tests indicates that on our scanner, a Hewlett Packard Scanjet, dark images without automatic threshold control enhance the classification process.

A preliminary scan at 6:1 compression (*i.e.*, 50 dots per inch) is used to reproduce a crude image on the monitor screen. The operator then uses a mouse to click the upper left and lower right of a rectangle enclosing the staffs to be analyzed at once. When all the rectangles have been identified, the scanning itself can proceed. The final scan is at 300 dots per inch and results in a rotated run-length encoded file.

2. Classifier Program

Most of the time is spent on classification. Whereas the input is a run-encoded rotated image of a few staffs, the output is a text file with the following format items:

- the staff number
- left side of component (in pixels)
- right side of component (in pixels)
- vertical position of component using *DARMS* representation
- a component identifier, as close to *DARMS* code as feasible

The classifier program performs many functions, but the main three, discussed below, are these:

> A. Staffline identification and removal
> B. Component identification and classification
> C. Beam/chord classification

A. STAFFLINE REMOVAL

While in many kinds of image analysis the isolation of components can proceed in a straightforward way, in musical scores the stafflines connect many objects and render them interpretable. For this reason, we concentrate on components with some black pixels between the stafflines. The identification of the stafflines is also essential for the *DARMS* encoding of the components [*DARMS* specifies vertical heights rather than pitches]. We find this to be the most frustrating part of optical music analysis. We err on the side of excess by dropping parts that are common both to stafflines and other objects. This is a tradeoff which is forced by our design decision to use a one-pass classifier, a restriction placed upon us by our meager hardware memory resources. The classifier sweeps along the staff, removing stafflines. As connected components are identified, they are classified, written to the output file, and released from memory.

Our staffline removal algorithm basically performs a correlation of the current line and the next line in the left-to-right scan, and if a long thin element is near a current staffline, it is associated with the staffline, and the position of the staffline is adjusted. We assume only that stafflines belonging to a common staff are parallel and that the total number of stafflines is a multiple of five. These staffline-like elements are shown in light grey on the screen, and the other pixels are shown in white. When the staffline elements are terminated (usually because they bump into components such as barlines, etc.) they are removed from memory.

Although the staffline removal algorithm is rugged, the starting position is, of course, important. The program initially knows neither the number nor the position of the stafflines. However, when it is determined that the number of short runs is a multiple of five, the program stops, beeps, and displays what it thinks are the stafflines. The operator may agree and save the information or disagree and press a key that gives the number of staffs (currently an integer from 1 to 9). In this second case, the program is told the position of the first and last of the five stafflines of each staff. Occasionally initial clefs may be accidentally omitted. The effect is small relative to the difficulty encountered in accurately identifying C clefs, which have a large number of different presentations.

B. COMPONENT ANALYSIS

A connected component analysis is carried out simultaneously with staffline removal. If a connected component—a set of pixels, all of which are connected—exceeding a size and position threshold is found, it is displayed in green on the screen. The tentative *DARMS* classification, including vertical position, is presented, again in green. The operator indicates whether to save, change, analyze (for beams and/or chords), or delete the component. In the case of a change, the prompt turns from green to red, and the operator simply types in the *DARMS* representation.

In the beam/chord analyzer, the component is rotated in memory, and the stemlines are identified much as the stafflines are identified. These stemlines are displayed in yellow, and the *DARMS* code associated with each stemline, which is based on a connected component analysis made when the stemlines are removed, is presented to the operator, who may save, change, or discard them. The remaining connected components are classified as beams or notes, and this determines the *DARMS* representation. A *DARMS* comment is applied to each of these components, indicating that they are all part of the same beamed or chorded component. In addition, the stem direction, the note duration, and the beaming are indicated. Since most notation programs will perform beaming automatically, and beaming is unnecessary for MIDI files, there is some redundancy in this information. We find that the beaming information is useful, however, in the editing of the *DARMS* code.

Since several measures cannot fit in one display, whenever a barline is identified, the screen is refreshed, moving that barline to the left side of the screen.

The classification of the components uses features which include and extend those presented by Prerau: the size of the bounding rectangle, the relative position of the top and bottom pixels (used to discriminate sharps, flats and naturals), the width at the middle in a vertical and horizontal position, the density of the component compared to the bounding rectangle, and the number of holes. The features are normalized to the staffline spacing.

C. FEATURE DATA

The features are stored by giving upper and lower bounds for the position features. A distance measure based on deviance from these bounds, the number of holes, and the density is used to classify the component. This information may be used to fine-tune the feature table. It may be customized for a particular musical source or class of printing.

Special utilities operate on a subsidiary output file which contains the features for all the components. The utility analyzes all of these files appearing in a subdirectory, prints out the maximum and minimum values for the features as well as the mean and standard deviations, and displays them on the screen. This information may be used to update the feature data.

3. Sort/Syntax Program

The output from the classifier is not in order. What is desired is a sort by staff, and then by position in the staff. The comments related to beam/chord number are stripped at this stage. Certain syntax simplifications are made. Notes appearing at the same time are (optionally) clustered to form a chord. The notes appearing at the same time are ordered from long duration to short. Dots appearing after an F-clef are dropped, double dots before a barline are merged into a repeat sign, dots above notes form staccato marks, and dots after notes are used to lengthen durations. Sharps and flats appearing at the beginning, if they are in the proper sequence, form a key signature.

Logical problems with the handling of beamed notes within *DARMS* require the use of linear decomposition, the creation of separate tracks of information to accurately represent nonhomophonic textures (for example the presentation of soprano and alto parts on a single staff). We have found it difficult to automate linear decomposition, even though we do retain stem directions. It seems preferable to drop the beaming information completely and restore it with the notation program.

4. *DARMS* Interpreter

The *DARMS* interpreter provided by Brinkman (1990) is used to assign absolute time values to all *DARMS* events. The *MusicReader* interpreter also assigns note volumes intelligently. The output may be displayed and analyzed. The interpreter is perhaps most useful in checking the syntax of the *DARMS* code.

5. MIDI Filemaker

A translation to Standard MIDI files enables the data to be used with most sequencers and notation programs. The MIDI files are also valuable for data verification.

The *DARMS* interpretation and MIDI file conversion utilities are supported by an assembly language editor (available as shareware) in which error messages are displayed with the lines of text in the editor, facilitating correction.

Program Performance

Program performance varies with the source material. Generally speaking, the scanning of single-line music with quarter notes or eighth notes, beamed sixteenth and thirty-second notes, and unbeamed chords is flawless. Individual sixteenth- and thirty-second notes are harder to identify because of the tails. Rests that occur in staves containing only one part are usually recognized; they can be troublesome in multipart music on one staff. Because of the ambiguous nature of white space, half notes and whole notes are difficult; they are currently recognized about 70 percent of the time. Either the staffline goes though them, and they look like quarter notes or quarter noteheads, or they are between stafflines and they become split into two components.

Clef recognition is difficult. The C-clef is most problematical, followed by the F-clef; the G-clef is usually recognized. Finally, beam/chord components with a multiplicity of stemlines going to one component are often misclassified, usually by presenting too many elements on each stem.

Despite these limitations, many of which are due to the poor quality of the starting images, we feel that such an analysis is always more efficient than encoding a work in *DARMS* alphanumerically, especially since the manually encoded *DARMS* file will need to be checked anyway.

Some deficiencies in the current program are inherent in the approach, while others are readily remedied. The problem of fragmentation of components owes to the use of the one-pass staffline removal algorithm. Its importance varies with the repertory. It would be a significant obstacle to a repertory containing a preponderance of half and whole notes, such as hymns. The problem of multiple stems attached to a single notehead is one of music representation. It should be capable of solution, perhaps using graph-based methods. The current program does not recognize text, but we are implementing a template-matching algorithm that may help. The text algorithm may be useful for the classifier as well.

Hardware enhancements would include porting to other popular workstations, such as the Macintosh, NeXT, and Sun SparcStation, and testing with hand-held scanners.

The system is now available for use, and user feedback would be much appreciated.

References

Brinkman, Alexander. *Pascal Programming for Music Research*. Chicago: University of Chicago Press, 1990.

Dydo, Stephen. "Data Structures in 'The NoteProcessor'," *Proceedings of the International Computer Music Conference, 1977* (Urbana: University of Illinois, 1977), pp. 311-16.

Merkley, Paul, and William F. McGee. "Optical Scanning of Music," *Computers and the Humanities*, May 1991.

Prerau, David. "*DO-RE-MI*: A Program that Recognizes Music Notation," *Computers and the Humanities*, 9/1 (1975), 25-29.

Further Information: William F. McGee, Nepean DSP Services, 73 Crystal Beach Drive, Nepean, Ontario, Canada K2H 5N3; tel.: (613) 828-9130; e-mail: *mcgee@citr.ee.mcgill.ca*. Paul Merkley, Department of Music, University of Ottawa, Ottawa, Canada K1N 6N5; tel.: (613) 564-9239; fax: (613) 564-5643; e-mail: *merkley@acadvm1.uottawa.ca*.

Music Score Recognition:
Problems and Prospects

The problem of recognition of music scores has much in common with the processing of other types of documents (mechanical engineering drawings, circuit diagrams, maps, and texts containing conventional English characters, Chinese and Japanese characters, and mixed alphanumerics and graphics [Yamamoto 1993]). Not only are they all binary (black and white) images but they also contain a mixture of line segments, characters, and domain-specific symbols. Current thinking in the document recognition community seems to agree on several key points, namely that no one recognition technique is going to solve the recognition problem for cases such as those listed above, that context will play a significant role in any successful recognition system, and that it would be useful to have not only databases of typical documents but also appropriate models of image degradation for use in system development and testing. It is interesting to note that some work on seemingly black and white originals makes use of the grey-scale image in order to direct the thresholding process and thereby create a better approximation to the symbol shapes in the image (Roach 1988, Yamamoto 1993).

While line-finding is a fundamental process in the graphic analysis of many categories of binary image, music is unique in making use of sets of five roughly horizontal, parallel, and equidistant lines as its reference grid. Another shared problem is that of touching symbols. Text annotations of circuit diagrams and engineering drawings sometimes touch the objects to which they refer; maps frequently contain touching or intersecting symbols. Music could be said to have this characteristic but to a greater degree because most symbols will touch or be superimposed upon the stafflines and, even after symbol isolation (staffline recognition), symbols which touch or are superimposed will probably remain.

It should be remembered that the first work in the field, undertaken in the late 1960s and early 1970s, was severely limited by hardware (Pruslin 1967, Prerau 1970). Now that computers commonly have sufficient storage capacity to handle large quantities of data (an 8.5" x 11" page digitized at 300 dots per inch [d.p.i.] requires about 1 MByte of storage) and enough processing power to undertake recognition tasks involving such quantities of information, music score recognition has become purely a software problem. Scanners capable of producing binary images at 300 or more d.p.i. and sophisticated music notation programs are now widely available and these provide the other ingredients necessary for the development of an integrated music score recognition system.

General Problems in Music Recognition

The music fragment shown below will be used to illustrate some of the significant problems involved in attempting to develop algorithms which can read music notation. It is important to emphasize that such algorithms need to be generally applicable in order to be truly useful. It is easy to make assumptions about scores early on in the development phase which turn out to be untrue upon examination of a wider range of repertories. This is not purely a criticism of music score recognition research but seems applicable to work on the other forms of binary image (circuit diagrams, etc.) recognition, where assumptions are sometimes made in modelling the structure of symbols which turn out to be inadequate when faced with the degraded images which exist in the real world. This is particularly the case in industry, where the automatic conversion into electronic form of old and deteriorating documents is often of particular interest precisely because the paper-based originals are of poor quality and are therefore reaching the end of their useful life.

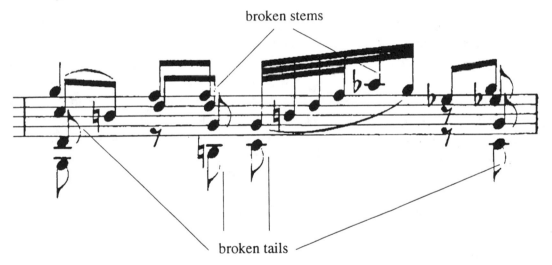

Example 1. J. S. Bach: an extract from the *Sonatas and Partitas for Unaccompanied Violin* (Dover Edition; after original engraving of 1894 by Breitkopf und Härtel).

Some of the basic requirements of a score recognition system include coping with variations in the following image parameters:

> 1. The size of original. Pocket scores may not have to be read by an automatic system but a reasonable requirement would encompass sparse instrumental parts with 6 or 8 staves per page, up to full orchestral scores. Staff height may vary between, say, 6 and 12mm.

2. The **rotation** of the original (the stafflines may be straight but not horizontal).

3. The **bowing** of stafflines. This is sometimes present in the original due to the printing process but may be introduced by the use of a hand scanner to acquire the image or by an intermediate photocopying stage.

4. The presence of **noise** in the image (either black specks, often referred to as "salt and pepper" noise, or dropouts, *i.e.*, white patches in symbols which should be solid black as well as slight variations along supposedly straight edges due to quantization).

5. **Discontinuities** such as breaks in stafflines or notestems (see Example 1).

6. Digitizing **resolution** (commonly 300 d.p.i.).

7. The music symbol **font**.

To put these requirements in context, it should be noted that omnifont text recognition in a range of sizes, in particular with touching characters, is still a current research topic (Yamamoto 1993). In comparison, score recognition requires coping not only with a range of music sizes, fonts, and distortions but also with the superimposition of symbols, not to mention the additional need for a built-in omnifont, size-independent character recognition facility which understands text underlay. Also, the above list does not include what is probably the most difficult problem in score recognition, *i.e.*, dealing with superimposed symbols, although it is also a complex process to extract implied information after symbol recognition has been achieved. This is amply illustrated by Example 1 with its varying number of voices, superimposed beamed groups, and staggered simultaneities. A more detailed discussion of the above parameters follows.

Specific Problems

1. Size

In order to process images of varying size, all measurements which are made on the image need to be relative rather than absolute. This is commonly achieved in current systems by normalizing all dimensions with respect to the vertical distance between adjacent stafflines. The other significant issue relating to size is the loss of symbol detail which occurs in some small scores. This leads to problems for the recognition engine which are similar to those produced by some instances of noise, poor-quality original pages where symbols are fragmented, or low resolution digitizing.

The use of multiple recognition modules, at least one of which would use context, is a possible solution in order to produce a "best fit" recognition result for an input image. It would also seem promising to undertake iterative recognition processing, perhaps in conjunction with a cost-function to direct results towards such a "best fit," albeit somewhat daunting to implement. This bears similarity to the annealing process for automatic layout of printed music described by Byrd (1980).

2. Image Rotation

It is reasonable to assume that the original will only be rotated slightly, at most, especially if a sheet-fed scanner has been used, but it is important to realize that only slight rotation is needed in order to render useless those staffline-finding algorithms which rely on finding horizontal lines. Also, some rotation may be present in the original image, so regardless of positioning relative to the scanning element, rotation is still a factor. The technique for staffline-finding must therefore include pre-processing to rotate the page, where necessary, or otherwise take account of rotation in dealing with line fragments. This issue is linked to the following parameter because stafflines cannot be assumed to be straight either (whether horizontal or not), so the staffline-finding process is forced to use a piecewise technique which permits bowed line fragments.

3. Staffline Distortion (Bowing)

Curvature in music score images, particularly of stafflines, is a source of difficulty for algorithms which assume that lines are straight. The human vision system has little difficulty in accommodating such distortions, so the widespread nature of the problem is perhaps not widely realized. Bowing can also be introduced by the scanning process, for instance if a hand scanner is used (see Example 2), or by photocopying the original prior to scanning.

Example 2. J. S. Bach: extract from the Flute Sonata in E Minor (Bach Gesellschaft; acquisition by hand scanner at 300 d.p.i.).

4. Noise (Dirt)

Noise in the input image takes various forms. Common examples are the black specks which appear in white background areas of a score due to the printing process or variations in the reflectivity of the paper. These need to be ignored by the recognition system but care must be exercised because similar-sized black regions may, depending on the position on the page, constitute a faint duration dot or be the sole difference between an 'l' and a 't' in a string of text. Similarly, white specks may appear within a region intended to be solid black. These alter the structure of the region and also reduce the effectiveness of a template-matching approach. Another effect which can be viewed as a form of noise is illustrated in Example 2, where lines vary in thickness. This is common, sometimes due to the quality of the original but often simply to the quantization process.

5. Discontinuities

This is a specific form of noise which manifests itself in the form of linebreaks (stafflines, stems, barlines, tails, etc. can all be affected) as illustrated in Example 1. This makes line-tracking, or other similar techniques which rely on line continuity, difficult and necessitates provision for traversing such gaps. It can also make the detection of line fragments more difficult if these are required to be unbroken.

6. Resolution

It is interesting to examine the amount of information which the human vision system is able to extract even from a low resolution image. The following illustrations show resolutions of 37.5, 75, and 150 d.p.i. with a progressive factor of four increase in the amount of data required to store each image.

It can be seen that the stafflines are readily identifiable even at the lowest resolution. A treble clef and a one-flat key signature followed by some beamed groups are also apparent, although a degree of uncertainty exists over most of the pitches. By the use of context, an eighth-note rest can be identified preceding the first beamed group.

As soon as the resolution is increased to 75 d.p.i., however, the extract can be read accurately, and 150 d.p.i. seems perfectly adequate for recognition purposes (thus making 300 d.p.i. appear excessive, particularly in view of the fact that it requires 16 times the quantity of data used by the 75 d.p.i. image).

37.5 dots per inch resolution

75 dots per inch resolution

150 dots per inch resolution

7. Font Variation

The wide variation in music symbols due to different fonts should be apparent from a typical selection of material from assorted publishers (Fujinaga 1988, p. 78). A score recognition system has to make its decision as to which symbol is present based on appropriate font-independent parameters. For instance a full-size treble clef will normally have a loop extending above the staff and a tail below the staff regardless of its slope, stroke width or height. Similarly, a bass clef will have two dots on either side of the F-line regardless of the ornateness of its main body, although detecting these dots may not be a trivial task.

Conclusion

In summary, some of the parameters which make music score recognition such a difficult problem have been presented. Progress has been made in coping with some of these variables, but current systems are still limited in scope. Also, it is still an open question how much information should be included in the output data file. This depends on whether it is just the musical content of the original which is being extracted or if it is also important to retain appearance, *i.e.*, the precise placement and style of symbols

References

Blostein, Dorothea, and Henry S. Baird. "A Critical Survey of Music Image Analysis" in *Structured Document Image Analysis*, eds. Henry S. Baird, Horst Bunke, and Kazuhiko Yamamoto (Berlin: Springer-Verlag, 1992), pp. 405-34.

Byrd, Donald. "Music Notation by Computer." Ph.D. dissertation, Indiana University, 1980.

Carter, Nicholas P. "Automatic Recognition of Printed Music in the Context of Electronic Publishing." Ph.D. dissertation, University of Surrey, 1989.

Carter, Nicholas P. "A New Edition of Walton's *Facade* Using Automatic Score Recognition" in *Advances in Structural and Syntactic Pattern Recognition*, ed. Horst Bunke (Singapore: World Scientific, 1992), pp. 352-362.

Carter, Nicholas P., and Roger A. Bacon. "Automatic Recognition of Printed Music" in *Structured Document Image Analysis*, eds. Henry S. Baird, Horst Bunke and Kazuhiko Yamamoto (Berlin: Springer-Verlag, 1992), pp. 456-65.

Fujinaga, Ichiro. "Optical Music Recognition Using Projections." M.A. thesis, McGill University, Montréal, 1988.

Prerau, David S. "Computer Pattern Recognition of Standard Engraved Music Notation." Ph.D. dissertation, Massachusetts Institute of Technology, 1970.

Pruslin, D. H. "Automatic Recognition of Sheet Music." D.Sc. dissertation, Massachusetts Institute of Technology, 1967.

Roach, J. W., and J. E. Tatum. "Using Domain Knowledge in Low-level Visual Processing to Interpret Handwritten Music: An Experiment," *Pattern Recognition*, 21/1 (1988), 33-44.

Yamamoto, K., ed. *Proceedings of the Second International Conference on Document Analysis and Recognition (ICDAR '93), Tsukuba Science City, Japan. October 20th-22nd*. IEEE Computer Society Press, 1993.

Further information: Nicholas P. Carter, Department of Physics, University of Surrey, Guildford, Surrey GU2 5XH, England, UK; tel.: +44 483/300800; fax: 483/300803; e-mail: *N.Carter@ph.surrey.ac.uk*.

How Practical is Optical Music Recognition as an Input Method?

Over the academic year 1992-3, Nicholas Carter, a leading researcher in the field of optical recognition of printed music, was in residence at the Center for Computer Assisted Research in the Humanities. Since the Center has been at work for almost ten years in the development of electronic representations of musical works, the circumstances were conducive to running a fairly well controlled test of the efficiencies of optical input vis-à-vis the CCARH standard input. This test was run in December 1993.

The Two Approaches

Carter's recognition program is designed to work with *SCORE* notation software. That is, after the score is converted to a bitmapped image, the recognition software attempts to identify objects and arrange these into a *SCORE* input file. The file is then converted to a *SCORE* parameter file, from which a musical score is printed. Errors are then corrected and the score is reprinted.

The CCARH system (*MuseData*; see pp. 11-28) involves realtime entry of pitch and duration through an electronic keyboard, syntax checking of this input, alphanumeric entry of information not enterable from a musical keyboard (articulation, dynamics, text underlay, grace notes and ornaments, basso continuo figuration, etc.), and proofreading, editing, and reprinting of printed scores. Proof-hearing also plays a major role in the Center's data verification process, but since no such operation was included in the optical recognition test, we discounted it in quantifying the performance of each approach.

Although in the test that was run a common goal—the replication of a single Haydn symphony—was pursued, there is one overall difference between the systems that could have a dramatic effect on more extensive comparison. *SCORE* is designed solely to capture and replicate an existing score. As an input process in its own right, it is not intended to facilitate assembly of a score from parts or other more varied approaches to acquisition. *MuseData* software can work from a score or from single parts or even from quite disheveled manuscript sources to a representation that supports not only notation but also sound output and certain kinds of analytical pursuits. The combination of *SightReader* plus *SCORE* has been aimed from the beginning at republication of preprinted material, whereas *MuseData* has from the beginning been aimed at the storage of musical information in a format hospitable to many and varied uses. Since files are organized by system and page in *SCORE*, the original format is replicated exactly in the recreation. This is not generally true for *MuseData*, which is organized by part and movement. Layout can, however, be altered in both systems.

The Music

The music on which this test was run was the Breitkopf und Härtel edition (1907) of Haydn's Symphony No. 1 (1759). The work was selected and photocopies for both contestants were made by Dr. Carter.

The work is generally laid out on three systems of six staves each to a page. There are six parts:

(1) Oboes 1 and 2
(2) Horns in D 1 and 2
(3) First violin
(4) Second violin
(5) Viola
(6) Violoncello and bass

There are three movements:

1. A *Presto* in cut time	5 pages
2. An *Andante* in 2/4	2.5 pages
3. A *Finale* (also marked *Presto*) in 3/8	2.5 pages

The oboes and horns are omitted in the second movement, which is laid out with five four-stave systems to a page. Page 8 contains two four-stave systems (end of the *Andante*) and two six-stave systems (start of the *Finale*). The second and third movements are in binary form. The outer movements are in D Major, while the *Andante* is in G Major.

Although the work is one of the musically simplest orchestral pieces by Haydn, it is not free of notational complexities. These include triple stops, abbreviation signs, grace notes, triplets, and trill signs in the string parts; polyphonically differentiated passages on the oboe staff; single notes with opposing stems on the horn staff; and so forth. Dynamics indicators, staccatos, ties, slurs, rehearsal numbers, and repeat signs are also present. In the main, however, the work consists principally of eighth and sixteenth notes, with some quarter, half, and whole notes and their corresponding rests.

The graphic images, while exhibiting many of the phenomena cited in preceding articles, were of generally good quality in that they are clear, with good contrast of black and white.

Quantitative Results

Because the unit of measure in *SCORE* is the page while in *MuseData* it is the movement, direct comparison of elapsed time was not immediately possible. We converted the *SightReader* page times to movement times by making the following assignments: times for pp. 1-5 = Movement 1 (*Presto*); times for pp. 6, 7, and half of p. 8 = Movement 2 (*Andante*); times for half of p. 8 plus pp. 9 and 10 = Movement 3 (*Finale*).

As an input method, *SightReader* has only two stages—(1) image acquisition (TIFF) and conversion to a *SCORE* input file and (2) screen editing of the provisional score. The *MuseData* acquisition process is considerably more involved and requires a total of 10 steps—three (Stage 1) devoted to pitch-and-duration acquisition and syntax checking and seven (Stage 2) devoted to merging parts, printing a draft score, correcting it, and reprinting it. Some of these steps are very short and their times are reported only in summary fashion.

The following respective timings (reported in hours, minutes, and seconds) were reported:

Movement	TIFF --> SCORE	Hand-editing	Total
Presto	0:05:49	5:46:00	5:51:49
Andante	0:04:55	2:24:05	2:29:00
Finale	0:02:24	1:34:05	1:36:29
Total	0:13:08	9:44:10	10:07:18

Table 1. Input (*SightReader*) and editing (*SCORE*) for the Haydn Symphony No. 1.

Movement	Stage 1	Stage 2	Total
Presto	1:55:00	4:24:00	06:19:00
Andante	1:20:00	2:52:00	04:12:00
Finale	1:05:00	2:04:00	03:09:00
Total	4:20:00	9:20:00	13:40:00

Table 2. *MuseData* input (Stage 1) and editing (Stage 2) times for the Haydn Symphony No. 1.

When the *MuseData* figures are consolidated to resemble the two steps in the *SightReader/SCORE* process (Table 3), then it becomes apparent that the *MuseData* editing time is marginally faster, but the original acquisition time is inevitably much slower, since it represents realtime performance, part by part, movement by movement.

Example 1. Beginning of the first movement of Haydn's Symphony No. 1
(*MuseData* reconstruction).

Example 2. Beginning of the third movement of Haydn's Symphony No. 1 (*MuseData* reconstruction).

System	Input	Editing	Total
Sight/SCORE	0:13:08	9:44:10	10:07:18
MuseData	4:20:00	9:20:00	13:40:00
Difference	4:06:52	0:24:10	03:32:42

Table 3. Comparison of *SightReader/SCORE* and *MuseData* systems of input.

It appears that efficient recognition is powerless to speed editing. One question that prospective users of recognition software must assess for themselves is whether they are prepared to make the same commitment of time to the editing process after optical music recognition as they do without it.

Qualitative Results

Judging the aesthetic quality of the output is entirely subjective. *SightReader* output resembles the materials shown on pp. 136-7. We reproduce the first pages of the first and third movements of the Haydn symphony from the *MuseData* printing system as Example 1 and 2.

As for accuracy, we originally took both "editions" to have been brought to the level of 100% accuracy. For the *SightReader* approach, accuracy consists of complete fidelity to the original material. This goal was achieved. For *MuseData*, however, accuracy consists of a faithful reproduction modified, as conditions warrant, to produce a fully sensible and workable set of information to be used for diverse applications. Frances Bennion and Ed Correia from CCARH found two errors in the Breitkopf edition related to the non-cancellation of accidentals. One case is given in Example 3. Numerous questions of visual grammar—ambiguous slurs, and so forth—also were encountered.

In the end, users will need to decide for themselves what level of data verification is required for their applications. A publisher wishing only to reprint a score may consider it unwarranted to proofread the original material before scanning. A performer working from an erroneous part or score or a MIDI file listener would undoubtedly prefer corrected material.

An overriding concern is that since *SCORE* is a model of completeness in the information that it represents, users of a scanning program that provides output to a simpler scheme, such as MIDI, or of limited sets of features (by excluding white notes, for example) must expect to spend a significantly greater amount of time in postprocessing than was the case in either instance here.

Example 3. Bars 74-77 of Movement 1 (*Presto*) of Haydn's Symphony No. 1.
In Bar 74 the final note for second violins (Staff 4) was not marked with a
natural in the original edition.

Our test narrowly avoided the inclusion of spurious material (an error that is unlikely
to occur except through the use of scanners). When the symphony was photocopied for
the participants, two pages of another Haydn symphony in the same meter strayed into
the stack of pages representing the Finale. The scanning program was completely
indifferent to this material, but the live data entry specialists found the abrupt change of
key and simultaneous reduction in the number of parts, from 6 to 5, disconcerting. They
investigated and discovered the error. This necessitated revising the results for
SightReader, which originally reported 12 pages of material and an addtional 66 minutes
of processing and editing time, and rerunning the *MuseData* test for the *Finale*; the
material was of course more familiar the second time.

The moral is obvious: technology, however sophisticated, is no substitute for
common sense. For the moment, scanning programs don't investigate; they simply scan.
Even within the domain of manual input, the eye can be deceived. This is why we
regard proofhearing as an essential step in the process of data verification. Old editions
have their share of errors and notational anomalies. Since so much effort is required to
encode musical data in large quantities, the additional human intelligence required to
rectify these seems well worth providing.

We expect all of the systems represented here to improve dramatically over time. We also expect optical music recognition to become practical for printing and analysis applications in due course. In these, as well as in sound applications via MIDI, the user's error tolerance and time available for the necessary postprocessing will determine the point at which use of the technology becomes practical.

We wish to thank Nicholas Carter, Edmund Correia, Jr., and Frances Bennion for participating in this experiment.

CCARH is willing to make available to other recognition software developers copies of the materials used in this comparison for the purpose of evaluating the performance of their programs.

Musical Notation Software

The Twentieth Century

Resource List

New Programs

Notation Software for Twentieth-Century Music

The recent publication of a collection of short piano pieces by contemporary American composers, *Various Leaves* (Fallen Leaf Press, Berkeley, 1992, music typesetting by Peter Simsich using *SCORE*), inspired us to tackle new music for the first time. In making four selections to distribute to the 80 developers on our list, our intent was to steer a course between the most conventional styles and some highly idiosyncratic notation that might defeat all but the most advanced programs. We may have been unnecessarily cautious: virtually all who responded included at least one setting from these pieces. As in years past, some developers reported using this opportunity to expand the capabilities of their programs, adding the requisite features or symbols.

In Donald Aird's "The Good News Service," a multitude of ties, some typographically awkward, need care in placement to avoid unduly confusing the performer. Diamond-shaped notes in Bar 39 indicate the silent exchange of these keys from the left to the right hand in preparation for use of the sostenuto pedal. This passage is actually much easier to execute than it may seem at first glance!

In the absence of barlines, the judicious spacing of notes and rests in "Blue Again" from Robert Basart's *Slow Pictures* becomes critical in clarifying the rhythmic divisions for the pianist. Details of articulation can easily get lost—the short dash over the first grace note in the upper staff was overlooked by many. Another unusual feature here and in the following example is the joining of two or more angled beams to indicate acceleration or deceleration within a group of notes.

Texture becomes less complicated in Herbert Bielawa's "Just Add Water"; in this fragment, the two hands never play simultaneously. Tonal variety is created by gradually adding resonance: first, by sustaining only the circled notes for the length of the slurs, then, by observing the pedal marks normally. These alternate with an initial "dry" reading as the lettered sections (five in all) are repeated and combined according to a prescribed plan. The engraver must therefore provide large letters, pause marks, circles, and verbal instructions.

The requirements for David Chaitkin's "Prelude" were possibly the least troublesome of this assignment. Distinguishing the three degrees of pedal and the unambiguous placing of dynamic detail were handled quite adequately by all who submitted a setting.

In honor of the sesquicentennial of his birth (1843), a fragment of Edvard Grieg's piano piece "Brudefølget drager forbi" ("The Bridal Procession Passes By"), Op. 19, No. 2, was suggested as a more traditional alternative to the contemporary pieces. Surprisingly, relatively few settings of this excerpt were received. Perhaps the less familiar music posed a more interesting challenge to our contributors, although a few did admit that the Grieg gave them more headaches. The accidentals resulting from notating an F major passage in four sharps, combined with constantly changing clefs, grace notes, an abundance of fingering numbers and other symbols, create a very tight squeeze for the typesetter.

We remind our readers that the contributors are not required to duplicate the exact layout of our examples. They are free to choose the number of measures per system and the spacing of staves and systems, and even to shorten the excerpts somewhat in order to meet our space restrictions. Further reduction is often necessary on our part to allow for margins and headers.

Illustrations from Regular Contributors

The numbered illustrations are arranged (1) alphabetically by composer and (2) alphabetically by the surname of the contributor. Illustrations are unretouched. Printer designations identify the specific configuration used to produce the example. Most programs can interface with several printers and some run on multiple platforms, but the results are not necessarily uniform. The originating hardware is indicated in this listing.

Donald Aird: "The Good News Service" (1992), second part.

1. Excerpt distributed	[*SCORE*]
2. Macintosh	*Finale 3*
3. Macintosh	*NoteWriter*
4. Acorn Archimedes	*Philip's Music Scribe*
5. IBM PC	*The Copyist*
6. Macintosh II	*Graphire music printing system*
7. Sun SPARCstation	*MusE*

Robert Basart: "Blue Again" from *Slow Pictures* (1992).

8. Excerpt distributed	[*SCORE*]
9. IBM PC-AT	*COMUS*
10. Atari Mega ST4 or TT	*Amadeus*
11. Acorn Archimedes (PC)	*Philip's Music Scribe*
12. UNIX workstation (NeXT)	*CMN (Common Music Notation)*
13. IBM PC	*The Copyist*

Herbert Bielawa: "Just Add Water" (1992).

14. Excerpt distributed	*[SCORE]*
15. Macintosh	*Finale 3*
16. Atari Mega ST4 or TT	*Amadeus*
17. Macintosh	*NoteWriter*
18. Erato workstation	*Erato Music Manuscriptor*
19. Acorn Archimedes	*Philip's Music Scribe*
20. IBM PC	*Personal Composer for Windows*
21. NeXT workstation	*CMN (Common Music Notation)*

David Chaitkin: "Prelude" (1992).

22. Excerpt distributed	*[SCORE]*
23. Macintosh	*Finale 3*
24. Acorn Archimedes (PC)	*Philip's Music Scribe*
25. NeXT workstation	*CMN (Common Music Notation)*
26. IBM PC	*The Copyist*
27. Macintosh II	*Graphire music printing system*

Edvard Grieg: "Brudefølget drager forbi" ("The Bridal Procession Passes By"), Op. 19, No. 2 (1871).

28. Excerpt distributed	[Typeset]
29. IBM PC-AT	*COMUS*
30. NeXT	*NoteAbility*
31. IBM PC	*Personal Composer for Windows*
32. NeXT	*CMN (Common Music Notation)*
33. Macintosh II	*Graphire music printing system*
34. Sun SPARCstation	*MusE*

Free choices:

35. J. K. Randall (Macintosh)	*Nightingale*
36. Karol Szymanowski (Erato workstation)	*Erato Music Manuscriptor*

Gallery of Examples

Illustration 1
Donald Aird: "The Good News Service," second part,
As shown in *Various Leaves* (Berkeley: Fallen Leaf Press, 1992).

*Note: while the left foot holds the sostenuto pedal (S.P.) in this movement, the right foot can cross behind it to activate the una corda pedal when required.

Excerpt sent to software developers.

Illustration 2 (Aird)

Contributor: Claire Dolan
Product: *Finale 3*
Running on: Apple Macintosh

Output from: LaserMaster's Unity
Size as shown: 75% of original

*Note: while the left foot holds the sostenuto pedal (S.P.) in this movement,
the right foot can cross behind to activate the una corda pedal when required.

Illustration 3 (Aird)

Contributor: Keith Hamel   Output from: NeXT LaserPrinter
Product: *NoteWriter*   Size as shown: 84% of original
Running on: Apple Macintosh

*Note: while the left foot holds the sostenuto pedal (S.P.) in this movement, the right foot can cross behind it to activate the una corda pedal when required.

Illustration 4 (Aird)

Contributor: Philip Hazel

Product: *Philip's Music Scribe*

Running on: Acorn Archimedes (PC)

Output from: Apple Laserwriter

Size as shown: 100% of original

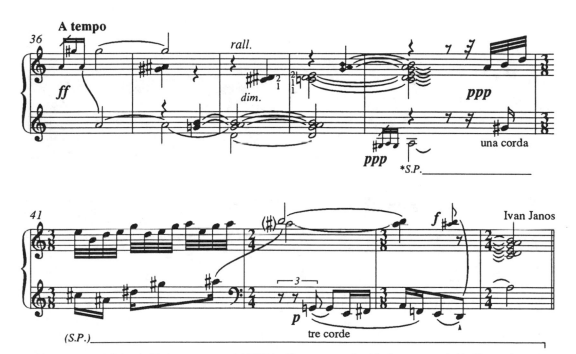

*Note: while the left foot holds the sostenuto pedal (S.P.) in this movement, the right foot can cross behind it to activate the una corda pedal when required.

Illustration 5 (Aird)

Contributor: Crispin Sion
Product: *The Copyist*
Running on: IBM PC compatibles

Output from: HP LaserJet 4M
Size as shown: 70% of original

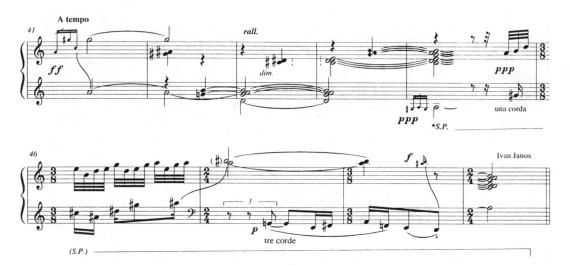

*Note: while the left foot holds the sostenuto pedal (S.P.) in this movement, the right foot can cross behind it to activate the una corda pedal when required.

Illustration 6 (Aird)

Contributor: Alan Talbot

Product: *Graphire* music printing system

Running on: Apple Macintosh II

Output from: Agfa Accuset 1000 (3000 dpi)

Size as shown: 87% of original

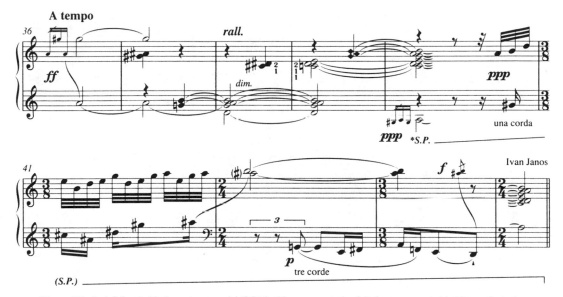

*Note: while the left foot holds the sostenuto pedal (S.P.) in this movement, the right foot can cross behind it to activate the una corda pedal when required.

Illustration 7 (Aird)

Contributor: Rolf Wulfsberg
Product: *MusE*
Running on: Sun SPARCstation (Unix)

Output from: Linotype L-300
Size as shown: 100% of original

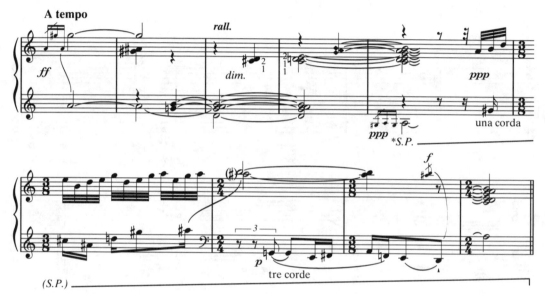

*Note: while the left foot holds the sostenuto pedal (S.P.) in this movement, the right foot can cross behind it to activate the una corda pedal when required.

Illustration 8
Robert Basart: "Blue Again" from *Slow Pictures*
As shown in *Various Leaves* (Berkeley: Fallen Leaf Press, 1992).

Excerpt sent to software developers.

Illustration 9 (Basart)

Contributor: John Dunn
Product: *COMUS* music printing software
Running on: IBM PC-AT

Output from: HP LaserJet +
Size as shown: 90% of original

Illustration 10 (Basart)

Contributor: Wolfgang Hamann
Product: *Amadeus*
Running on: Atari TT, ST4

Output from: Linotronic 300
Size as shown: 80% of original

Illustration 11 (Basart)

Contributor: Philip Hazel

Output from: Apple Laserwriter

Product: *Philip's Music Scribe*

Size as shown: 83% of original

Running on: Acorn Archimedes (PC)

Illustration 12 (Basart)

Contributor: Bill Schottstaedt
Product: *CMN (Common Music Notation)*
Running on: NeXT workstation (Unix)

Output from: NeXT LaserPrinter (400 dpi)
Size as shown: 85% of original

Illustration 13 (Basart)

Contributor: Crispin Sion

Product: *The Copyist*

Running on: IBM PC compatibles

Output from: QMS PS 800+

Size as shown: 70% of original

Illustration 14
Herbert Bielawa: from "Just Add Water"
As shown in *Various Leaves* (Berkeley: Fallen Leaf Press, 1992).

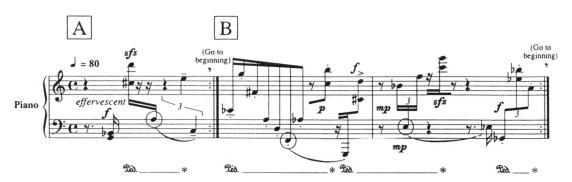

(Before each repeat pause briefly.
When playing through do NOT pause.)

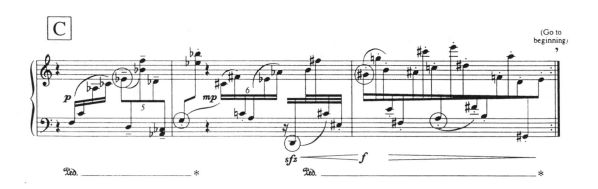

Excerpt sent to software developers.

Illustration 15 (Bielawa)

Contributor: Claire Dolan

Product: *Finale 3*

Running on: Apple Macintosh

Output from: LaserMaster's Unity

Size as shown: 70% of original

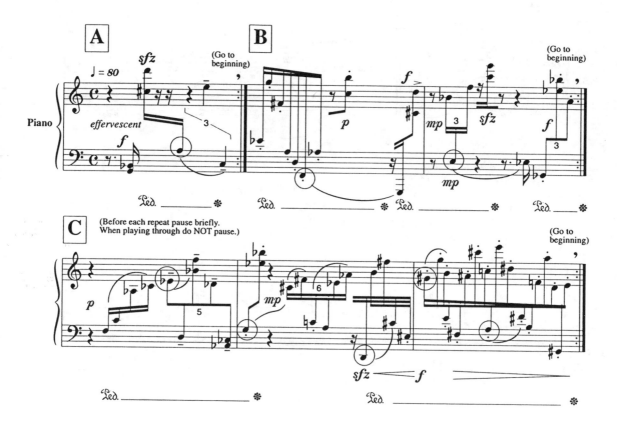

Illustration 16 (Bielawa)

Contributor: Wolfgang Hamann
Product: *Amadeus*
Running on: Atari TT, ST4

Output from: Linotronic 300
Size as shown: 80% of original

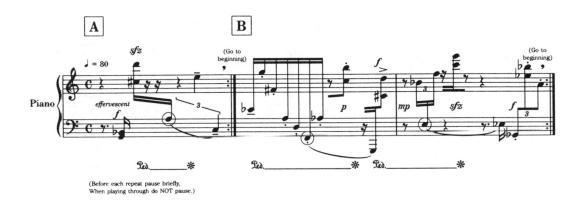

(Before each repeat pause briefly,
When playing through do NOT pause.)

Illustration 17 (Bielawa)

Contributor: Keith Hamel
Product: *NoteWriter*
Running on: Apple Macintosh

Output from: NeXT LaserPrinter
Size as shown: 91% of original

Illustration 18 (Bielawa)

Contributor: John C. Hawkins

Product: *Erato Music Manuscriptor*

Running on: Erato workstation

Output from: HP LaserJet II

Size as shown: 82% of original

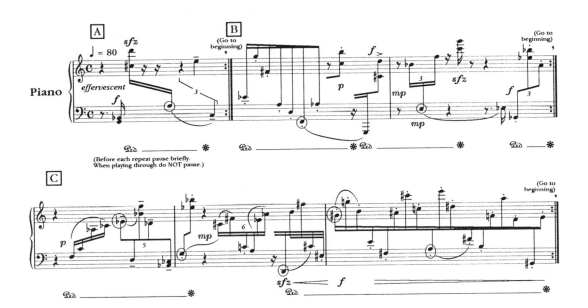

Illustration 19 (Bielawa)

Contributor: Philip Hazel
Product: *Philip's Music Scribe*
Running on: Acorn Archimedes (PC)

Output from: Apple Laserwriter
Size as shown: 88% of original

(Before each repeat pause briefly.
When playing through do NOT pause.)

Illustration 20 (Bielawa)

Contributor: Susan Miller

Product: *Personal Composer for Windows*

Running on: IBM PC compatibles

Output from: HP LaserJet 4

Size as shown: 85% of original

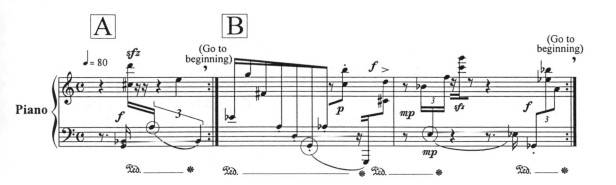

Illustration 21 (Bielawa)

Contributor: Bill Schottstaedt
Product: *CMN (Common Music Notation)*
Running on: NeXT workstation (Unix)

Output from: NeXT laserprinter (400 dpi)
Size as shown: 85% of original

Illustration 22
David Chaitkin: "Prelude"
As shown in *Various Leaves* (Berkeley: Fallen Leaf Press, 1992).

Excerpt sent to software developers.

Illustration 23 (Chaitkin)

Contributor: Claire Dolan

Product: *Finale 3*

Running on: Apple Macintosh

Output from: LaserMaster's Unity

Size as shown: 70% of original

Illustration 24 (Chaitkin)

Contributor: Philip Hazel

Product: *Philip's Music Scribe*

Running on: Acorn Archimedes (PC)

Output from: Apple Laserwriter

Size as shown: 83% of original

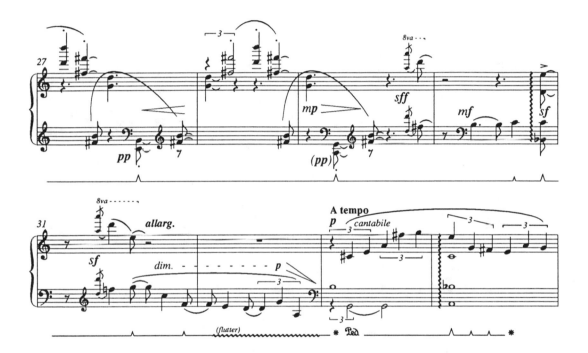

Illustration 25 (Chaitkin)

Contributor: Bill Schottstaedt   Output from: NeXT laserprinter (400 dpi)
Product: *CMN (Common Music Notation)*   Size as shown: 85% of original
Running on: NeXT workstation (Unix)

Illustration 26 (Chaitkin)

Contributor: Crispin Sion   Output from: HP LaserJet 4M
Product: *The Copyist*   Size as shown: 70% of original
Running on: IBM PC compatibles

Illustration 27 (Chaitkin)

Contributor: Alan Talbot   Output from: Agfa Accuset 1000 (3000 dpi)
Product: *Graphire* music printing system   Size as shown: 87% of original
Running on: Apple Macintosh II

Illustration 28
Edvard Grieg: "Brudefølget drager forbi," Op. 19, No. 2 (1871).

Excerpt sent to software developers.

Illustration 29 (Grieg)

Contributor: John Dunn

Output from: HP LaserJet+

Product: *COMUS* music printing software

Size as shown: 85% of original

Running on: IBM PC-AT

Illustration 30 (Grieg)

Contributor: Keith Hamel   Output from: NeXT LaserPrinter
Product: *NoteAbility*   Size as shown: 77% of original
Running on: NeXT workstation (Unix)

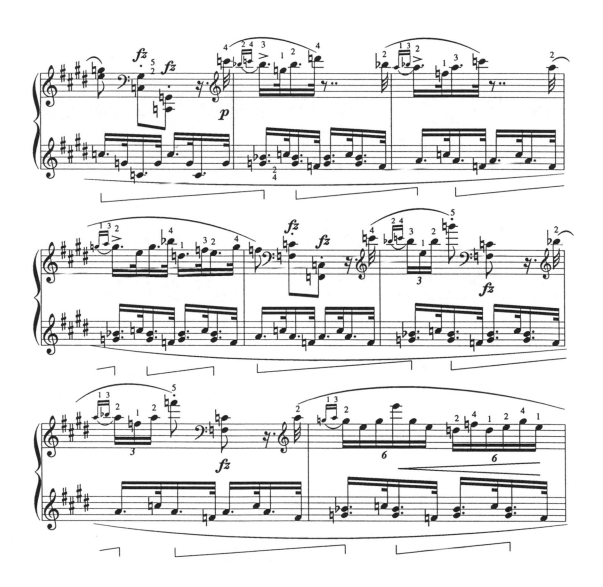

Illustration 31 (Grieg)

Contributor: Susan Miller   Output from: HP LaserJet 4
Product: *Personal Composer for Windows*   Size as shown: 82% of original
Running on: IBM PC compatibles

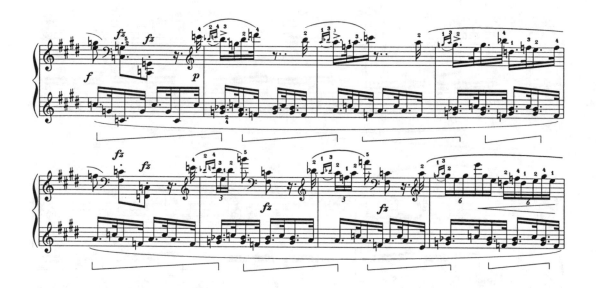

Illustration 32 (Grieg)

Contributor: Bill Schottstaedt
Product: *CMN (Common Music Notation)*
Running on: NeXT workstation (Unix)

Output from: NeXT laserprinter (400 dpi)
Size as shown: 85% of original

Illustration 33 (Grieg)

Contributor: Alan Talbot   Output from: Agfa Accuset 1000 (3000 dpi)
Product: *Graphire* music printing system   Size as shown: 80% of original
Running on: Apple Macintosh II

Illustration 34 (Grieg)

Contributor: Rolf Wulfsberg
Product: *MusE*
Running on: Sun SPARCstation (Unix)

Output from: Linotype L-300
Size as shown: 100% of original

Computing in Musicology

Illustration 35
Free choice—music by J. K. Randall

Contributor: Donald Byrd

Product: *Nightingale*

Running on: Apple Macintosh

Output from: Linotronic L-300

Size as shown: 82% of original

Engraver: John Gibson

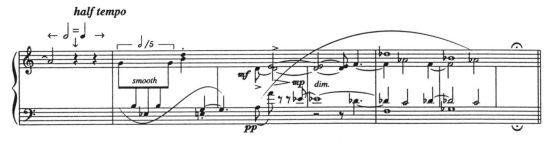

Excerpt from J. K. Randall: *3 for Piano* (Red Hook, NY: Open Space, 1991).

Illustration 36
Free choice—music by Karol Szymanowski

Contributor: John C. Hawkins

Product: *Erato Music Manuscriptor*

Running on: Erato workstation

Output from: HP LaserJet II

Size as shown: 77% of original

Excerpt from Karol Szymanowski: "Pieśni Muezina Szalonego" ["Songs of the Infatuated Muezzin"], Op. 42 (1918), No. 4.

Recent Contributors: A Resource List

This listing concentrates on systems that have been represented by illustrations over the past three years and incorporates definitions of terms needed to understand the accounts given. Many additional systems have been cited in earlier issues. Listings for several developers (and their products) who have not contributed in recent years can be found in the 1990 volume of *CM*, pp. 62-73. Music printing programs advertised in popular music magazines are listed here if they have a demonstrated capability for handling classical music of moderate complexity.

Amadeus. Amadeus Music Software GmbH, Lindenberg 81, D-82343 Pöcking, Germany; tel.: +49 8157/5234; fax: +49 8157/5333. Technical support is available from Wolfgang Hamann; tel.: +49 89/669678; fax: +49 89/669579. This product, originally developed by Kurt Maas, is commercially available for the Atari Mega ST4 or TT using a Unix-like operating system. It is currently being ported to PCs running Linux; other Unix versions for the PC may follow. Both alphanumeric and MIDI input are supported, the latter facilitating acoustical playback. Most data are stored as ASCII files. Screen editing is provided. Output (for dot matrix and laser printers, plotters, and phototypesetters) is scalable to a resolution of 1000 dots per inch.

C-Lab Notator. See **Notator**.

Calliope. *Calliope* is a Unix-based printing program under development by William Clocksin, Computing Laboratory, University of Cambridge, New Museums Site, Pembroke St., Cambridge, CB2 3QG, UK; e-mail: *fennel@cl.cam.ac.uk*. A graphics-based program, *Calliope* has extensive capabilities for printing early repertories. See pp. 216-20.

CMN (Common Music Notation). *CMN* is a LISP-based common music notation system developed by Bill Schottstaedt,

Center for Computer Research in Music and Acoustics, Stanford University, Stanford, CA 94305; tel.: (415) 725-3580; e-mail: *bil@ccrma.stanford.edu*. This package is available free at the anonymous FTP site *ccrma-ftp.stanford.edu* in the file *pub/cmn.tar.Z*. Its input is a LISP expression using various standard musical names (*e.g.*, *c4* for Middle C, *e* for eighth-note, etc.). Its output is normally a *PostScript* file. *CMN* currently uses the Adobe *Sonata* font for clefs and other complicated symbols. It is aimed primarily at composers using Heinrich Taube's *Common Music* [see p. 73], and in that connection it can also import Standard MIDI Files. It can be used as a stand-alone Western music notation program but is a bit tedious to operate in that mode. Limited technical support is now offered by the developer at the above number and e-mail address.

Comus. Comus Music Printing and Publishing, Armthorpe, Tixall, Stafford ST18 0XP, England; tel.: +44 785/662520. The proprietary music printing program developed by John Dunn for this firm uses *DARMS* encoding of data and produces high resolution, device-independent graphics output. Systems of unlimited size, including percussion staves and strophic text lines, are supported, with part extraction in any desired combination. Designed originally for a Unix environment, versions have run on a variety of machines from mainframes to an IBM PC-AT (the current host). A DOS version is now available, and the source code (in *C*) is also supplied on a trust basis. A previewer (VGA driver) and a graphics-based *DARMS* editor are also part of the system.

The Copyist III. Dr. T's Music Software, 124 Crescent Rd., Suite 3, Needham, MA 02194; tel.: (617) 455-1454; fax: (617) 455-1460. Three versions of this commercial program for Atari, Amiga, and IBM PC compatibles are offered by Dr. T's. "III" is the most comprehensive version and the one best suited to academic applications. MIDI input and output are supported. Files, which are edited graphically on the screen, can be converted to TIFF and EPS files. Output to *PostScript* and *Ultrascript* printers as well as the Hewlett Packard LaserJet Plus and plotters is supported. *The Copyist* interfaces with a number of popular sequencer and publishing programs. The developer is Crispin Sion. Also illustrated in 1990 and preceding years.

Dai Nippon Music Processor. Dai Nippon Printing Co., Ltd., CTS Division, 1-1 Ichigaya-kagacho 1-chome, Shinjuku-ku, Tokyo 162-01, Japan; fax: +81 03-3266-4199. This dedicated hardware system for the production of musical scores was announced six years ago and illustrations were provided in 1988, 1990, and 1991. Input is alphanumeric. Screen editing is supported. Output files can be sent to MIDI instruments, to *PostScript* printers, to a Digiset typesetter, or to the *Standard Music Expression (SMX)* file format used in music research at Waseda University. Kentaro Oka, the author of a recent article [*cf. CM 1991*, p 20] on the use of Standard Generalized Markup Language for music documents, is the current manager.

DARMS is an encoding system that originated in the 1960's. Various dialects have been used in several printing programs, including *MusE*, *The Note Processor*, *Comus*, and systems developed at the State University of New York at Binghamton by Harry Lincoln and at the University of Nottingham, England, by John Morehen. A sample of the code is shown on p. 129.

Dean, Jeffrey. The Stingray Office, 16 Charles Street, Oxford OX4 3AS, England; tel./fax: +44 865/727060; e-mail: *oxcomray@vax.oxford.ac.uk*. Jeffrey Dean, a registered user of *Finale*, is a musicologist specializing in the 15th and 16th centuries who now works as a freelance book designer and typesetter. Examples of his work, displaying the typefaces he has designed in order to reproduce all the symbols of mensural notation, can be found in recent and forthcoming publications of Oxford University Press. Rather than make the set of typefaces available commercially, Mr. Dean hopes that scholars wishing to use them in their publications will ask him to do the typesetting. He may make available bitmapped fonts so that musicologists may use the characters in low resolution.

ERATO workstation. See under *Music Manuscriptor*.

ESTAFF. A notation program for single-voiced melodies. It automatically translates any file encoded in *ESAC* into conventional staff notation, and is compatible with the Essen *MAPPET* files (now numbering some 13,000 documented melodies). *ESTAFF* can also be used to write notes onto a blank staff, to design custom musical graphics, and to convert Western notation into Chinese Jianpu notation [see p. 223] with automatic text underlay. Available free by license to interested researchers. For more

information please contact Helmut
Schaffrath at the Universität Essen, FB-4
Musik-Postfach, W-45131 Essen 1,
Germany; e-mail: *JMP100@VM.HRZ.UNI-ESSEN.DE*.

Finale. Coda Music Technology, 6210
Bury Drive, Eden Prairie, MN 55346-1718;
tel.: (612) 937-9611; fax: (612) 937-9760;
technical support tel.: (612) 937-9703.
Finale has a broad range of capabilities
related to music transcription and printing.
It is available in both a Macintosh and a
Windows/PC version. This year's contribution is from the Macintosh program.

Graphire music printing system.
Graphire Corporation, 4 Harvest Lane, PO
Box 838, Wilder, VT 05088; tel.: (802)
296-2515; e-mail: (AppleLink):*graphire*.
This is a professional music typesetting
program (as yet unnamed) for the
Macintosh. It is entirely new software
based on the technology developed at New
England Digital for the Synclavier Music
Engraving System (shown in prior years).
It is designed for use in a wide variety of
commercial and academic situations. It
handles all conventional notations as well as
several less common ones, such as shape
notes, tablature, and numerous modern
notational practices. Input is accomplished
by typing, MIDI step time, or standard
MIDI file transcription. The system
supports output to any *PostScript*-
compatible imaging device.

L.M.P. [Laser Music Processor] Prima.
TEACH Services, 182 Donivan Rd.,
Brushton, NY 12916; tel.: (518) 358-2125.
A demo file of Version 3.2 (*LMP32P.ZIP*)
is available on CompuServe. In this
program for IBM PC compatibles note
entry is by computer keyboard, mouse,
standard MIDI file transcription, or MIDI
device. More than 400 symbols are
available. Dot-matrix printers can produce

draft and high-resolution (240 d.p.i.)
output. A driver for the Hewlett Packard
DeskJet is available as well as print-to-file
and *PC Paintbrush (PCX)* image-file
formats. Illustrated in 1991.

Lime *[Lippold's Music Editor]*. Lippold
Haken, CERL Sound Group, University of
Illinois, 103 S. Mathews #252, Urbana, IL
61801-2977; fax: (217) 244-0793. Soft-
ware distribution is being handled by Jodie
Varner, Electronic Courseware Systems,
Inc., 1210 Lancaster Drive, Champaign, IL
61821; tel.: (800) 832-4965; also (217)
359-7099; fax: (217) 359-6578. This
Macintosh version of the *Interactive Music
System* music printing program was
developed by Haken (University of Illinois)
and Dorothea Blostein (Queen's University,
Kingston, Ontario). For a free
demonstration copy of *Lime* by FTP over
Internet, send electronic mail to *L-Haken@uiuc.edu*. A description of *Lime*'s
music representation system is also
available to the public. Illustrated in 1991.

MusE (formerly *A-R Music Engraver*). A-
R Editions, Inc., 801 Deming Way,
Madison, WI 53717; tel.: (608) 836-9000;
fax: (608) 831-8200. A commercial
version of the music typesetting system
used by this publisher for its own editions
and musical examples for academic journals
is now available by license. Tom Hall is
the principal developer. This version of the
program, for the Unix operating system,
uses the *OpenWindows* interface on the Sun
SPARC and SPARC-compatible workstations with a high resolution monitor
(1600 x 1280). Music input is done
alphanumerically with a modified version of
DARMS; files may be created on other
systems before processing and editing on
the workstation. *PostScript* images may be
imported to the music page, and likewise,
MusE can create *EPS* graphics files for
export into other programs. A music

notation library developed by A-R and multiple text fonts created by Mergenthaler are cross-licensed and available for use with the program. *PostScript* printers and typesetters are supported.

MuseData™. CCARH, 525 Middlefield Rd., Ste. 120, Menlo Park, CA 94025; tel.: (415) 322-7050; fax: (415) 329-8365; e-mail: *XB.L36@Stanford.Bitnet*; *XB.L36 @Forsythe.Stanford.Edu*. The Center's music representation system supports the development of electronic transcriptions and editions of a large quantity of musical repertory, chiefly from the sixteenth through the eighteenth centuries [see p. 27]. A corollary music printing system, developed by Walter B. Hewlett, has been used to produce performing scores of major works of the eighteenth century. Examples appear on pp. 160, 161, and 163.

Music Engraver (formerly **HB Music Engraver**). Ken Johnson, Music Engraver, 7725 E. 14th Ave., Denver, CO 80220; tel.: (303) 329-6468. This printing program runs on the Apple Macintosh and produces output for *PostScript* printers. Input is alphanumeric and utilizes redefinition of the QWERTY keyboard. No direct contribution has been received in recent years. For examples of what the program can do, see the contributions of Don Giller (300 W. 106th St. #22, New York, NY 10025; tel.: (212) 663-0515; CompuServe 71310,561) in 1991 and 1992.

Music Manuscriptor. Erato Software Corp., PO Box 6278, Salt Lake City, UT 84152-6278; tel.: (801) 328-0500. This commercially available program operates as part of an integrated workstation for composition and orchestration. Setup requires a PC compatible, a digitizer tablet or mouse, MIDI device, math chip, and laser printer (HP-compatible, including 11x17). Super-VGA and large format displays up to 2400 x 1600 pixels are available. Pitches are entered and edited as MIDI data. Output is to *TIFF* files. There is also 32-channel audio playback and an early music feature. Recent innovations include a user-editable lexicon of annotative text (labels) for rapid placement. MIDI controls can be embedded within labels to affect program and graduated tempo changes during playback. A page layout editor provides desktop publishing controls for headers, footers, and margins with style sheet defaults.

MusicEase. Grandmaster, Inc., PO Box 2567, Spokane, WA 99220-2567; tel.: (509) 747-6773. This commercial product for IBM PC compatibles is primarily intended for on-screen assembly and editing of musical data, but it can also accept MIDI data in real time or step time. MIDI files may be imported and exported. Illustrated in 1991.

MusicProse. See *Finale*.

MusicTeX [also **MuTeX**] is a set of fonts developed by Angelika Schofer and Andrea Steinbach for music typesetting with the TeX document description language. The fonts and numerous printer drivers are available by FTP at several sites. Queries may be directed to Werner Icking, Gesellschaft für Mathematik und Datenverarbeitung mbH, Schloss Birlinghoven, PO Box 1316, D-5205 Sankt Augustin, Germany; tel.: +49 2241/142443; e-mail: *icking@gmd.de*. For examples of the code and the result see pp. 222-23.

MusScribe. See *NoteWriter II*.

Nightingale. Advanced Music Notation Systems, 13 Detroit Ave., Troy, NY 12180; e-mail: *don@cogsci.indiana.edu*. Don Byrd's Macintosh program for music notation has been made available by

Temporal Acuity Products, Inc., 300 120th Avenue N.E., Bldg. 1, Bellevue, WA 98005; tel.: (800) 426-2673; technical support line: (206) 462-1007; fax: (206) 462-1057. *Nightingale* primarily uses MIDI input but data may also be entered via the Mac keyboard and mouse. Output may be edited graphically and further revised in popular desktop publishing programs. This year's free choice contribution was produced in 1991 by beta-tester John Gibson (a member of the University of Virginia faculty). *Nightingale* has also been tested extensively with both early and contemporary repertories by Tim Crawford at King's College, University of London.

Notator. C-Lab Software GmbH, Postfach 700303, D-2000 Hamburg 70, Germany; tel.: +49 40/694400-0. Now distributed in the US by Ensoniq Corp., PO Box 3035, Malvern, PA 19355; tel.: (215) 647-3930. The design intent behind this software package by Gerhard Lengeling and Chris Adam for the Atari ST series was to combine advanced sequencing and notational capabilities in one product. As such, it stresses flexibility of input (primarily MIDI), editing control, efficient performance-to-printed-page interface, and overall ease of use. For those chiefly interested in notation, a junior version called *Alpha* is available, with the main difference being in the sequencer. Illustrated in 1991.

The Note Processor. Thoughtprocessors, 584 Bergen Street, Brooklyn, NY 11238; tel.: (718) 857-2860; fax: (718) 398-8411; CompuServe: 73700,3475. A demo (*NOTEPR.ZIP*) and guitar fonts (*NPGUI. ZIP*) are available on CompuServe. Stephen Dydo's program for PC compatibles accepts both alphanumeric (*DARMS*) and MIDI input; data can be edited either through code revisions or on

screen with a mouse. Numerous dot matrix printers, inkjet, and laser printers are supported. The optional *Outline Option* produces *PostScript* files. Examples shown in 1992 and preceding years.

NoteAbility. CIUSA, 3208 West Lake St., Ste. 133, Minneapolis, MN 55416; technical support available from Gerard Schwarz, tel.: (612) 822-1604. This program, designed and written by Keith Hamel (see *NoteWriter* below), is in the final stages of development and should soon be available from CIUSA. It operates on any computer running the NeXTStep environment, allows a variety of input methods, and provides output to a wide range of laser printers and phototypesetters. *NoteAbility* has a page-oriented design: a score is set up according to a template specifying page size, initial number of systems on the page, staves and measures per system, etc. The music can be entered directly onto the page at any location and in any order.

NoteWriter II. Keith Hamel, School of Music, University of British Columbia, Vancouver, BC V6T 1W5, Canada; fax: (604) 822-4884; technical support offered by Dr. Hamel at tel. (604) 822-6308 or e-mail: *hamel@unixg.ubc.ca*. This commercial product for the Apple Macintosh is the heir of *MusScribe* (shown in 1988) and has been developed by Keith Hamel with a focus on avant-garde music and complex analytical requirements. *NoteWriter*, which is *PostScript*-compatible, is used to typeset musical examples in several scholarly and popular music journals. *QuickScrawl* mode permits users to draw freehand. Analytical examples submitted by a user, John William Schaffer, were shown in 1991.

Personal Composer for Windows. 3213 W. Wheeler St., Ste. 140, Seattle, WA 98199; tel.: (206) 524-5447; fax: (206)

524-5910; support line: (206) 524-4766. This program, originally developed by the late Jim Miller for the IBM PC line, has been released in an all-new version using *Windows 3.1*. Notation, MIDI sequencing, and printing have been integrated into one program with emphasis on ease of use for the novice. Several editing features facilitate page setup and layout as well as use with desktop publishing programs. Most popular sound boards are supported.

Philip's Music Scribe (PMS). 33 Metcalfe Road, Cambridge CB4 2DB, England; tel.: +44 223/334714 or +44 223/65518; e-mail: *P.Hazel@ucs.cam.ac.uk*. This commercially available program by Philip Hazel for the Acorn Archimedes computer uses alphanumeric input and produces *PostScript* files as its "top quality" output, though several other printers are supported. It runs on Acorn's proprietary RISC operating system, and displays the music on screen for proofreading exactly as it will appear on the page. Acorn products are currently available in the UK, Europe, Canada, Australia, New Zealand, and South Africa.

PMS, completely rewritten with many new features, has extensive capabilities for accommodating the needs of parts and scores derived from a common input file. Staves can be overlaid, permitting four-part choral music to be shown on two staves, for example. Any number of verses of text underlay and/or overlay can be accommodated. Up to eight parts can be played through the computer's sound system for proofhearing purposes. Some generalized drawing commands are also provided. Slur control is extensive and basso continuo

figuration is supported. All characters found in the *PMS* music font set are available for use in text strings.

SCORE. San Andreas Press, 3732 Laguna St., Palo Alto, CA 94306; tel./fax: (415) 853-9394. A demo (*SCORE.ARC*) is available on CompuServe. Leland Smith's *SCORE* program for IBM PC compatibles is now in use by many major music publishers. Translation programs to and from the *SCORE* format are also becoming numerous. The original input system is alphanumeric and requires separate passes for pitch, rhythm, and articulation. Several supplementary products provide other means of input. Output is to *EPS* files. Forty music fonts are available. Version 3.1 provides MIDI pitch input, automatic guitar tablature (with conversion option to lute tablature), 1200 guitar chord fingerings, and a library for user-designated musical terms. *MIDISCORWRITE*, a MIDI-to-SCORE transcription program, is available from New Notations, Unit 9, Down House, Broomhill Road, Wandsworth, London SW18 4JQ, England; tel.: +44 81/8715193; fax: 81/8773494.

Virtuoso. Musical notation represents one capability of this interactive music system developed for the Macintosh and PCs running *Windows*. An expert system provides the foundation for the product, which was announced late in 1992 from Virtuoso Software, Inc., 742 Dudley Avenue, Winnipeg, Manitoba, Canada R3M 1S1; tel.: (204) 452-0508.

Programs Not Previously Reported

Score Perfect Professional

Score Perfect Professional is a music notation program developed in the first instance for the Atari. German and English versions of screen menus are available. Various dot matrix, laser, and desk printers are supported with resolutions ranging from 180 to 360 d.p.i. Earlier versions of the program, by Michaelle Frey, have been available since 1990. Windows and Macintosh versions are nearing release. The screen views shown are from version 2.0. The most recent version is 2.1.

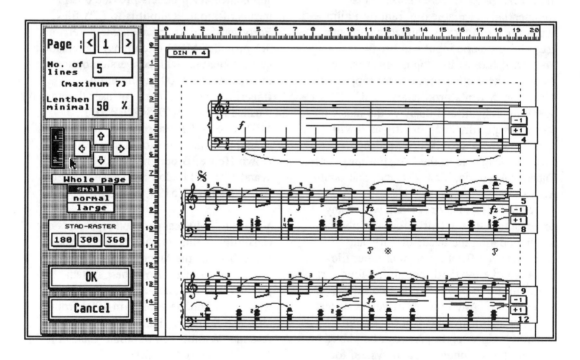

Score Perfect Professional: A page layout window.

Score Perfect Professional provides its own font, *SIGNUM II*, for printing. It also supports MIDI output through conversion to Standard MIDI files. Other features supported include text underlay, guitar tablature, polyphonic voice on one staff and support for European and American paper sizes (A3, A4, A5).

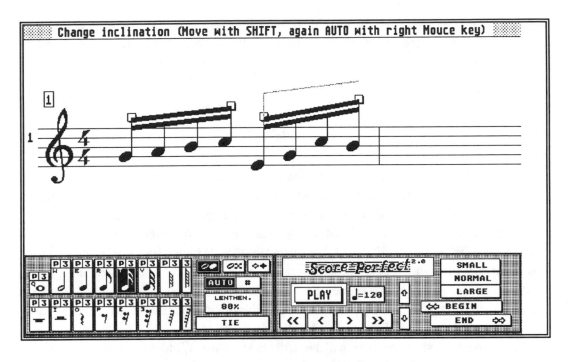

Score Perfect Professional: A beam editing tool.

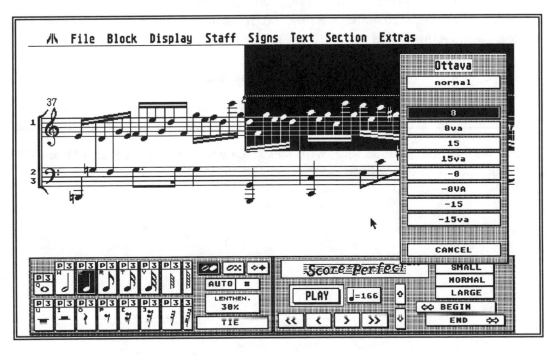

Score Perfect Professional: An octave transposition menu.

Further information on *Score Perfect Professional*: Michaelle Frey, Soft Arts, Postfach 12 77 62, D-10598 Berlin, Germany; or Niementzstrasse 47-49, D-12055 Berlin; tel.: +49 30/684 37 37; fax: +49 30/685 80 41.

capella 1.5

The DOS music printing program *capella*, Version 1.5, is designed for home and classroom use. It is easy to install and operate; the well-written manual includes a tutorial. Print quality is excellent, even on a nine-pin printer. *capella* offers a choice of input methods: (1) ASCII input using letter-names for pitches and integers for duration; (2) redefinition of the keyboard to simulate a piano (there is a template for this input method, which also "hears" durations); and (3) a Windows-like screen with good resolution and quick response (the refresh rate can be set by the user). Playback options include the PC loudspeaker, a Soundblaster-compatible card or a Roland-MPU-compatible or Soundblaster Pro MIDI interface.

Some existing shortcomings will be addressed in the Windows version, scheduled for release in the first half of 1994. These include lack of support for tuplets and stemless noteheads, presentation of polyphonic voices on one staff, and export of output to other programs (other than by screen capture). There is one scalable font for text (with German letters).

Report and illustration provided by *David Halperin*

Further information: Hartmut Ring, WHC Musiksoftware GmbH, An der Söhrebahn 4, 34318 Söhrewald, Germany; tel.: +49 5608/3923; fax: +49 5608/4651.

capella: Output from a dot-matrix printer.

The *Calliope* Music Notation Editor

Calliope is a music notation editor intended for rapid production of performance editions.   Most of the features of conventional music notation are supported. *Calliope*'s built-in placement and formatting knowledge frees the copyist from the need to specify precise placement of musical symbols.   The notation is never "frozen": notation is automatically reset each time the music is edited, assuring typographic consistency and professional quality results.   Also, *Calliope* provides uniquely flexible features required for early music editions: correct treatment of multi-verse underlay, figured bass, several kinds of lute tablature, and chant notation.

There are special provisions for the notation of early music (*c.*1560-1650).   This important period includes the golden age of English lute music, the madrigalists, the Italian "florid monody" and *seconda prattica*, and the explosive growth of church music under the influences of the Reformation and Counter-Reformation.   Early Baroque repertory is of renewed interest to performers and musicologists, as well as being a commercial growth area.

Calliope has been especially useful in the preparation of scores of florid vocal works, such as songs or motets, from the early seventeenth century.   This style is particularly interesting because it provides unusual challenges to the technology of automatic music formatting.   Works by such composers as G. P. Cima, Alessandro Grandi, Johann Kapsberger, Claudio Monteverdi, Biagio Marini, and Salomone Rossi as well as the opera *Sant'Alessio* by Stefano Landi have been printed in complete editions using *Calliope*.

Environment

Calliope, written in *Objective-C*, runs under all versions of NeXTStep above 2.1, available at this time only on the NeXT family of computers. A previous version of *Calliope*, written in *C*, ran under *X-Windows*, but this version is no longer supported.

Calliope uses a "what you see is what you get" style of interaction. It works at the conceptual level of the user's musical intentions.   In particular, most layout and formatting tasks are done automatically according to conventional notational practices. This frees the user from making detailed graphical adjustments, reduces the amount of time required to input and edit a score, and reduces the amount of training required to use the system. Scores are printed at a higher resolution than seen on the screen.

Other features include:

- Unique adjustment algorithms for automatic, musically correct formatting.

- A variety of page formatting and running title options are provided.

- Scores may be played back through the NeXT's built-in sound synthesizer.

- Musical excerpts may be exported as EPS or TIFF and pasted into other documents.

Limitations

Calliope is not the musical equivalent of a freehand drawing program, and therefore *Calliope* is not particularly suitable for the preparation of scores containing freehand notation such as may be found in modern avant-garde compositions, analytical diagrams, or advertising copy. Scores produced with *Calliope* may, of course, be imported into drawing programs if freehand notation is required.

Scores having as many as a dozen or more voices may be played back subject to the limitations of the NeXT computer's built-in music synthesizer. The playback facility is not intended to capture subtleties of musical expression or articulation, and thus is intended only for "proof-listening" and not for sequencing or public performance.

Design

Because *Calliope* is intended for professional quality music layout, some care has gone into the design of the music symbols and the "house style" implied by the default layout conventions and proportions. The standard music symbols are drawn from the *Sonata* font (developed by Adobe Systems Inc.).

The "French" (letter system) lute tablature font was designed after the style of the standard humanist hand used to cut the type for the vast majority of printed lute books published in England from the 1580s onward. See, for example, Robert Dowland's *Varietie of Lute Lessons* (1610).

The "Italian" (number system) lute tablature font was designed in the style of the early seventeenth-century Italian publishers of lute and theorbo tablature Ricciardo Amadino of Venice and G. P. Moscatelli of Bologna. Other early music notation was designed after the symbols used by the major European publishers of music in the years around 1600 such as Bartolomeo Magni and Alessandro Vincenti of Venice.

The chant notation was designed after the definitive *Graduale Sacrosancte Romanae Ecclesiae* and *Liber Usualis* compiled by the Solesmes community in the first few decades of the twentieth century. The default text font is *New Century Schoolbook*, often used in music typesetting because its relatively wide en-width suits verse underlay. [This sentence is displayed in the *New Century Schoolbook* font.]

To run *Calliope* it is necessary to install the *Sonata* and *Calliope* music fonts and the *New Century Schoolbook* text font. The *Calliope* font is included with the *Calliope* software, but the other fonts must be obtained from dealers.

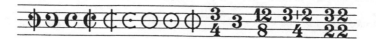

Calliope: Some possible time signatures.

Calliope: Use of double time signatures in a seventeenth-century canzonetta. Close placement is provided by an adjustment algorithm. Unlike many programs that using timing for error-checking, *Calliope* intentionally ignores the musical significance of a time signature.

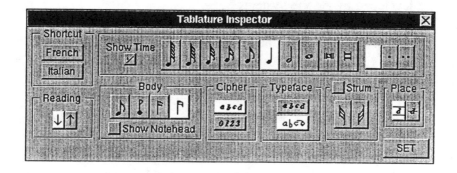

Calliope: The Tablature Inspector, a tool for lute tablature.

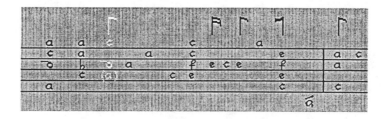

Calliope: A passage of lute tablature; each letter indicates a fret. The cursor is at "(a)" in the highlighted chord.

Calliope: chant notation.

Calliope: The Neume Inspector, a tool for specifying neumes and neume attributes.

References

Homewood, S., and C. Matthews. *The Essentials of Music Copying*. London: Music Publishers' Association, 1990.

Read, Gardiner. *Music Notation: A Manual of Modern Practice*. London: Victor Gollancz, 1985.

Smith, C. "The Art of Music Printing," *Royal Society of Arts Journal* (April, 1989).

Graduale Sacrosanctae Romanae Ecclesiae. Paris: Desclée, 1961.

Liber Usualis. Paris: Desclée, 1963.

Further information: William F. Clocksin, Computer Laboratory, University of Cambridge, New Museums Site, Pembroke Street, Cambridge CB2 3QG, England, UK; e-mail: *William.Clocksin @cl.cam.ac.uk*. A draft manual is available.

MusicTeX

MusicTeX (*MuTeX*, *et al.*) produces musical notation by adding object and parameter codes to the typesetting program *TeX*. One example of its use is provided by Helmut Schaffrath. Selections from the databases of ethnomusicological resources developed at Essen University have been published using *MusicTex*. Below is the *MusicTeX* file for the Chinese song "Da zhi Shange guo hengpai," which appears, with an English translation, on the following page.

```
\input u
\input mtex
\input vorschla
%\font\bog=slurdd16
%\chardef\bogen=\hex38
%\font\balk=beam16
%\chardef\bal=\hex33
\font\nor=cmr8 scaled \magstep0
\font\sarg=cmr7 scaled \magstep0
\font\sack=cmr6 scaled \magstep0
\font\jeck=cmr5 scaled \magstep0

\hsize 10 true cm
\vsize 26 true cm

\baselineskip 1.0\baselineskip

%\overfullrule=0pt
\mittg
\noindent
{{\mittt
54: Da zhi Shange guo hengpai   }\hfill{Shange
}}
\sn\no
\hfill{Jiangxi, Xingguo (Hanzu) }
\bn
\melodie{10.0 cm}{0.0 cm} %
{beliebig: }{ } %
{%
```

```
% ----------> PHRASE 1 ****************
\vio\D\meter2/4 %
\_{Ai}{\a7} %
{\def\beamlist{\\{1-2,}\\{1-2,}} %
\group{\\{\_{ya}{\s7}}\\{\_{}{\s4}}} %
    {\\{7}\\{4}} %
    \lbeam{1}{2} %
    \uslur{1}{2} %
\go} %
\_{lai}{\v6} %
\| %
\_{ai,}{\h7} %
\| %
} %
\arbeit{
\pfolur {225} {114}
}
\vskip -1.2 true cm

\melodie{10.0 cm}{0.0 cm} %
{}{} %
{%
```

MusicTex: print file header information and the first phrase of "Da zhi Shange guo hengpai".

54: Da zhi Shange guo hengpai Shange

Jiangxi, Xingguo (Hanzu)

beliebig:

Ai   ya   lai   ai,

Da zhi shan- ge (jiu) guo heng- pai,

Heng- pai lu shang (jiu) shi- ya (ya a ge) ya,

Xing le ji duo (jiu) shi- zi lu,

Mi ji xiao- de wo tong- zhi- ge

Zhuo lan ji- duo (jiu) he- cao (o huo) xie.

I sing a mountain song and walk along the mountain path;
there are overhanging rockwalls there.
How far I have already gone, stony the whole way!
Do you know, brother comrade,
how many straw sandals have been worn out?

MusicTex: Transcription of "Da zhi Shange guo hengpai" from Chinese Jianpu notation.

This process, involving the use of an IBM PC and an HP LaserJet 4, was used to produce all the music in Schaffrath's edition of *Einhundert Chinesische Volkslieder Begleitdiskette zum Buch* (Bern: Peter Lang, 1993).

MusicTeX is described in Angelika Schofer and Andrea Steinbach's dissertation, "Automatisierter Notensatz mit TeX" (Bonn: Rheinische Friedrich-Wilhelms-Universität, 1987).

Sibelius 7

Sibelius 7 is a program for the Acorn line of computers (Archimedes, A3000, A4000, and A5000 series). These are not available in the U.S. but are widely used in the United Kingdom and available in Europe. Supporters claim that the Acorn's operating speed greatly outdistances IBM PC-compatibles and Macintoshes. Sibelius's developers state that the speed of their program is further enhanced by its having been written entirely in assembly language; the screen may be redrawn in one-tenth of a second.

Sibelius can export EPS files that can be used on these computers and with image processing software. It also imports and exports Standard MIDI Files. Acorn computers can run IBM software under emulation. Input may be via mouse or MIDI keyboard. A dynamic image of the music is continuously available, as the input occurs, on the screen. Output devices supported range from dot matrix printers and ink jet printers to laser printers and Linotronic typesetters. Opus II music fonts are provided with the program.

Sibelius claims to incorporate an expert system for completion and placement of notational elements. It is designed for large, complex works and has been used for setting music by Satie, Lutosławski, and Peter Maxwell Davies among others. Many features in part/score setup, extraction, and transposition are automatic. A range of "house styles" is available by menu.

Documentation for *Sibelius* is couched in a slender but highly readable tutorial on musical notation.

Further information: Ben Finn, Sibelius Software, 4 Bailey Mews, Auckland Road, Cambridge CB5 8DR, England, UK; tel.: +44 223/302765. *Sibelius 7* is also available through New Notations, Unit 9, Down House, Broomhill Road, Wandsworth, London SW18 4JQ, England, UK; +44 81/871 5193; fax: 81/877 3493; e-mail: *100272.662@compuserve.com*.

La fille aux cheveux de lin

(The girl with the flaxen hair)

Sibelius 7: Opening of Debussy's "La fille aux cheveux de lin."

Wayne Cripps

Tab

Tab is a typesetting program for French and Italian lute tablature. *Tab* runs on all Unix platforms thus far explored and should run on any mainframe or PC that has a *C* compiler. The program is available, with easy installation instructions, by FTP from *sunapee.dartmouth.edu*. Free technical support is available from the author.

Music is entered as an ASCII text file with a word processor. Line 1 of "Scottish Hunt's Up," shown on the next page, could be input as

```
b,2. c- a,#4 a,x c,2 d,#2 c- a,x d,xa,b,2. c- a,#4 a,x c,2 d,#2 c-
a,x d xa,b,#2 a - d,x b,x d,2. d - d,#4 c,x d,2a,b
```

Alternatively, every set of items occurring between commas can be given on a separate line, without commas.

Tab converts the input code into a sort of generic printer format. To convert this format to something suited to a specific printer, the program *dvips*, which provides conversion to PostScript, is recommended. It is available at no cost. Previewer programs are available to display the output on the screen.

Tab is intended to produce legible tablature with an attractive appearance. Its features have been strongly influenced by Margaret Board's calligraphy. *Tab* produces proportional spacing based on the time value of the flags, which makes it easier to read. The program does not provide automatic line breaks, but in compensation users may put one phrase on a line. This requires judgment at a level that the computer can't make. One can vary the density of notes on the page by putting more or less on a line. Generally where there has been a choice between ease of use and appearance, a better appearance has been supported.

The possibility of a common tablature document exchange format is being explored. The author also moderates a lute discussion list. The subscription address is *lute-request@cs.dartmouth.edu*. The contribution address is *lute@cs.dartmouth. edu*. Currently there are about 100 subscribers.

Further information: Wayne Cripps, P.O. Box 677, Hanover, NH 03755; e-mail: *wbc@huey.dartmouth.edu*.

Tab: English tablature. The opening of "Scottish Hunt's Up," No. 18 from Jane Pickering's Lute Book.

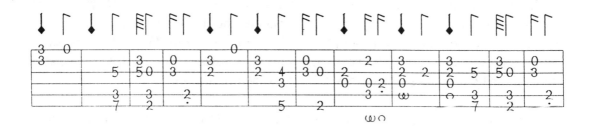

Tab: Italian tablature. One system from the "Padoana," No. 17 of the Capirola Lute Book.

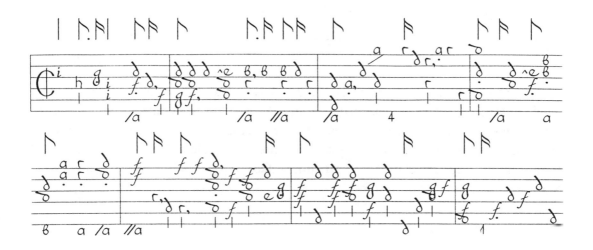

Tab: French tablature. From the allemande "Le Tombeau de Monseigneur le Prince de Conde par monsieur Gallot."

Frans Wiering

Lute Code: A *DARMS*-Based Tablature Code

The purpose of *Lute Code* is to facilitate the printing of lute tablatures with *The Note Processor* and to produce a rough, chordal (*i.e.*, non-polyphonic) transcription of the tablature. The code is used in combination with a program that converts *Lute Code* into *Note Processor DARMS* according to certain specifications (such as the tuning of the lute, and the key signature) made by the user. It has been in use since the summer of 1991.

Lute Code is intended mainly for lute music from the sixteenth and seventeenth centuries written in Italian tablature; it is also employed for French tablature of the same period.

In *Lute Code* the space code of each note token in *Note Processor DARMS* is replaced by a series of characters that represent the tablature chord. Theoretically, it can thus encode almost everything that is possible in *Note Processor DARMS*, while at the same time it shares its limitations. However, the principal musical attributes that are encoded are pitch and duration—so far as they are represented in the tablature.

Example 1a: Encoding for Ricercar 1 from Vincenzo Galilei, *Fronimo* (1584), Bars 1-6:

```
20-12Q 40-2-0E 52-20E. /
rS 52-4-2E 42--4S ---4 -2-3E /
2-44-2 -2 -45 ---42 /
00---4 ----2 -2--0 -0-3-4 /
-2-4-2 2-4 -45 7----7 /
45-2 52-20 +-34-2S 4 2E /
```

In tablature 1a the positions of the fingers on the neck of the lute are represented by numbers (10, 11 and 12 are encoded x, y and z). The lowest (written) symbol of each chord is encoded first. Hyphens are used for strings that are not played; those following the highest written note can be left out. Durations are indicated by the usual *DARMS* codes; "r" is a repeated chord; "+" a tied note (see Bar [=line] 6: here it prolongs the 5 of the preceding chord).

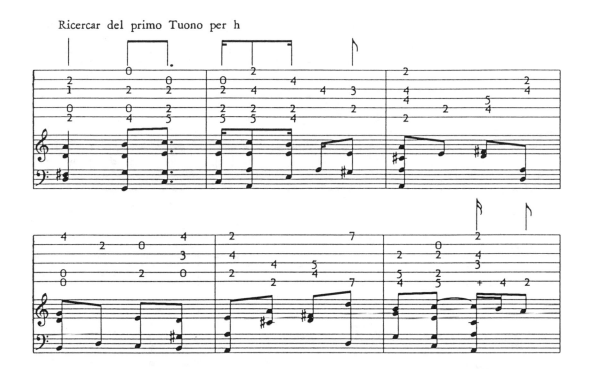

Example 1b. Tablature and transcription of Galilei's Ricercar 1, Bars 1-6, produced by *The Note Processor*.

Example 2a: Encoding for Denis Gaultier, "La Dedicasse," Bars 1-4:

```
a---:-abaQ.  ---aS --b ---aE e -cE.  --cS /
-abE a---:Q dE c --c ae --cS -e /
cE a: -a ---a ---c --b -cccE.  ---eS /
-e-|aE c -e --d a-:--eeQ ---eE ----a /
```

In Example 2a lowercase letters are employed instead of numbers. The ":" separates contrabass strings and ordinary strings. "|" is a symbol that indicates that notes should be played simultaneously.

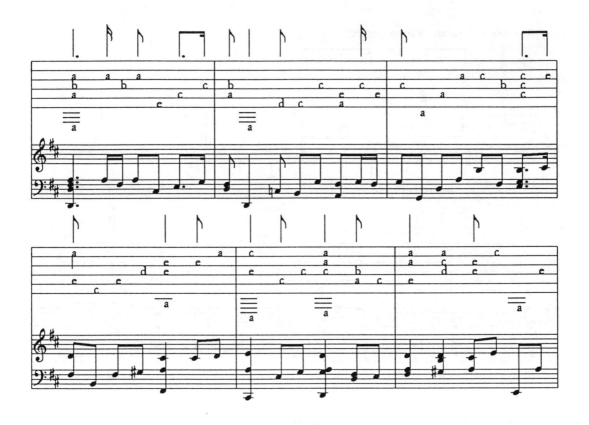

Example 2b.   Tablature and transcription of "La Dedicasse," Bars 1-6, produced by *The Note Processor*.

Further information: Frans Wiering, Instituut voor Muziekwetenschap, University of Amsterdam, Spuistraat 134, NL-1107 XL Amsterdam, Netherlands; e-mail: *WIERING@ ALF.LET.UVA.NL*.

Software and Data:

A Survey

Musical Software and Data Formats:
A Survey of Current Usage

We were curious to know how our readers use their computers in musical applications. Software designers often generalize from their own experiences, aptitudes, intuitions, and preferences, while users' choices are driven by perceived functionality in relation to specific, but highly varied, needs. These needs are often quite different from those imagined by software designers. Marketers are interested in users' opinions up to the point of sale, but for the readership we serve, there appears to be very little follow up on user satisfaction. We decided to find out what people are actually using rather than merely acquiring.

We constructed a simple ten-question survey not intended to win high marks for its conceptual sophistication. We distributed the survey to those on the CCARH mailing list and to the members of two U.S. academic societies—the American Musicological Society [AMS] and the Society for Music Theory [SMT]. A number of our overseas readers started replying by electronic mail. This encouraged us to circulate a revised version of the questionnaire electronically.

In the electronic version we fixed a few flaws and added a few items, which of course we cannot fairly tabulate, but we will pass on the general sense of the responses. Responses to the electronic survey were received from subscribers to the *Music Research Digest*, the *Early Music* listserver (*rec.music.early-music*), the *Opera America* listserver, the *comp.music* newsgroup, and the Society for Music Theory listserver. Since the questionnaires had to be signed in order to be tabulated, there was no chance of double submissions.

There is, however, a North American bias to the responses. This was moderated somewhat by the electronic mailing, the response to which came predominantly from Europe. If we were sophisticated statisticians, we would have been interested to break down the answers by continent, by constituency, and so forth. Instead we have broken them down by platform. The geographical bias should be kept in mind principally because the proportion of Macintosh users is considerably higher in the U.S. than it is elsewhere; conversely the Atari, which is barely used in the U.S., is in substantial use in several European countries.

Despite its haphazard sampling techniques, the survey elicited responses from an amazingly broad geographical range. Responses were received from Canada, Mexico,

Brazil, and Argentina; Norway, Sweden, and Denmark; France, Germany, Great Britain and Northern Ireland, the Republic of Ireland, the Netherlands, Belgium, Italy, Spain, Greece, Slovenia, and the Slovak Republic; India, Japan, Australia, and New Zealand. In all there were 352 responses. Of these, roughly 80% responded to the (first) printed version and the remainder to the (revised) electronic version.

General Observations

Platforms

The most unexpected finding of this survey, and one we did not anticipate in constructing it, is that for any given music application, a surprisingly large number of respondents are using more than one program.

Twenty-eight per cent are working on more than one platform, mostly frequent a Mac and a PC, but occasionally a Mac and a Unix workstation, or a PC and Unix, or some combination involving a mainframe. Among these respondents some are working on three platforms and a few are working on four. This augments the number of programs in use by a given user substantially. It also obscures preferences. Here is the overall breakdown of platform use:

Macintosh	62%
PC (DOS)	46%
Unix	18%
Atari	9%
Mainframes	4%
Amiga	1%

The Unix contingent may be subdivided as follows:

NeXT	10%
Sun	6%
Silicon Graphics	2%
Acorn	<1%

Since we did not anticipate such a large volume of multiple answers to a single question, we were unable to decipher preferences among those using multiple programs and multiple platforms. In most columns percentages totalling above 100% reflect multiple answers to single questions.

Applications Overview

All ensuing results are reported by platform because it is eminently clear that each platform has a distinct predisposition towards certain kinds of applications. Overall, respondents' use of computers is allocated as follows:

Sound applications	40%
Notation	62%
Music analysis	43%

However, the ordering of these varies with the platform, such that

- On the Macintosh the use of notational software was reported by 71% of respondents, with 51% citing analytical applications, and only 40% citing sound applications (a surprising lack, given the large number of sound programs that run on the Mac).

- On the DOS-based PC notational software is almost as popular (65%), but analysis is pursued less (33%) than on the Mac and sound applications are used less still (25%).

- Among the respondents using multiple platforms (often including Unix) and Unix-only users sound applications predominate (55%). These are followed closely by notation applications (52%) and analytical applications (46%).

In this and all other answers, respondents were generous with additional information. In the revised survey composition, teaching, and presentations were offered as additional choices. Including a number of write-ins on the first version, composition garnered an impressive 22%. We are unprepared to comment on the exact activities that the term encompasses. It appears to include everything from playing sequences to writing symphonies and from species counterpoint to sound synthesis.

Sound Applications

For many users of music applications, MIDI (the Musical Instrument Digital Interface) is the only acknowledged means of facilitating sound applications. MIDI's sole purpose is to enable communication between an electronic synthesizer and a computer. Its capabilities and limitations will be well known to most readers. Languages designed for timbral control flourish on Unix systems, yet their impact on personal computers remains slight. The responses we received to a question about means of sound interfacing and control are predictable. We acknowledge that the answers are not directly comparable, since one means of control may serve a different purpose from another. However. each tends to exclude the others. These are the results:

- Mac users of sound software are running 1.6 programs each. These include the following:

MIDI (interface)	55%
MAX (programming environment)	4%
Csound (representation for synthesis)	3%
Kyma (system for synthesis and control)	<1%

The MAX environment, developed by Miller Puckette at IRCAM (Paris), is offered by Opcode Systems. Kyma, developed by Carla Scaletti and Kurt Hebel at the University of Illinois, is sold by Platypus Systems.

Music Tracks and *Practica Musica* were the MIDI-based programs most frequently mentioned in write-in responses. Other programs in use for sound management are *Alchemy*, *Band-in-a-Box*, *Ed Sound*, *Performer*, *Sound Editor*, *Sound Tools*, *Sound Works*, and *Vision* as well as several programs for music notation.

- On the DOS platform, where less sound software is used, usage was reported as follows:

MIDI software	31%
Csound (PC)	4%
Sound Blaster	<1%

Cakewalk was the most frequently mentioned sequencer. DOS users of sound software are employing 1.3 programs.

- Among those working on multiple platforms, the following usage was reported:

MIDI software	72%
Csound	37%

Csound, developed in the early Eighties by Barry Vercoe at Massachusetts Institute of Technology, flourishes on Unix systems, most of which cannot handle MIDI.

Low levels of usage were also reported for *CMN* (Common Music Notation), *LIME*, *MAX*, and *AWI*. The first two are listed under the notation category; fuller commentary is in the music printing section. Besides *Cakewalk*, *Music Tracks Pro*, and *Vision*, voluntary mention was made of *Cubase*, *Presto*, and Turtlebeach software as well as the Bol Music Processor, a special-purpose program for the study of (Indian) tabla drumming. Users of sound software are employing 1.5 programs each.

All up, 53% of the respondents have some involvement with MIDI and 15% with *Csound*.

Notation Software

Notation software is almost as hardware-dependent as sound software, so composite figures are less meaningful than platform-specific figures. For the sake of completeness, we can report that the leading programs in use for music printing turned out to be these:

Finale (Mac and Windows)	50%
Professional Composer (Mac)	14%
SCORE (PC)	13%
Notewriter (Mac)	8%
Personal Composer (PC)	7%
Mosaic (Mac)	6%
MusicPrinter Plus (PC)	6%
Encore (Mac/Windows)	5%
Note Processor (PC)	5%
Nightingale (Mac)	4%
Notator (Atari)	4%

Figures for *Finale* include the economy-size *Music Prose*. *Mosaic* is an approximate successor to *Professional Composer* but, as a distinctly different program, is reported separately. It is clear that the ability to run on both the Mac and under Windows on the PC gave *Finale* a distinct advantage at the time the survey was run. Several other notation programs for the Mac have been or are about to be released in Windows versions, so these figures may be expected to change over the next year.

We were surprised by the strong showing for *Professional Composer*, which has not to our knowledge undergone any revision for several years; its publisher, Mark of the Unicorn, has put its energy into *Mosaic*. We think this means both that the original *Composer* program remains quite serviceable for many kinds of applications and that in a time of severe budgetary restraints, the purchase of new software for music notation may not seem justified. It may also mean that some respondents checked off everything they have used in the past ten years. We have no way of gauging the currency of each item in multiple answers to single questions.

1. Notation Software on the Mac

Those using only a Macintosh are running 2.5 notation programs. *Finale* appears to be a clear favorite, with 70% of Mac respondents reporting that they use it. What we are unable to determine is whether they are using it in preference to other programs loaded on their computers or in addition to them. We also acknowledge a few specious returns, in which the Mac was identified as the computer in use but the programs checked (*e.g.*, *MusicPrinter Plus*, *SCORE*, *et al.*) are not available on the Mac.

After *Finale,* the rates of utilization reported by Mac-only users are as follows:

Professional Composer	27%
NoteWriter	12%
Mosaic	10%
Nightingale	8%
Encore	5%
HB Music Engraver	4%
Music Prose	4%
Deluxe Music Construction Set	3%
LIME	3%
Concertware + MIDI	<3%

Receiving mention below the 2% level were *CuBase, Music Time, Music Shop*, and *Music Publisher* (now defunct). Three per cent of Mac users indicated use of *Personal Composer*, a program that runs only on PCs; 4% indicated use of *Notator*, which runs on Ataris. We are unable to determine whether these were mistaken for *Professional Composer* and *NoteWriter* or whether these Mac users function in work environments where they also use PCs and Ataris.

2. Notation Software for MS-DOS Machines

The distribution of programs is more level in the DOS world. Our survey did not make a distinction between Windows applications, which can be adapted readily from Mac software, and traditional DOS, from which migration to Windows is possible but migration to the Mac means writing a new program from scratch. Of the programs listed below, *Finale* and *Encore* run on DOS machines only under Windows. All the rest originated on traditional MS/DOS machines or migrated to them from mainframe computers. Several have Windows versions under development. DOS-only users reported the following rates of use:

Finale	27%
SCORE	23%
[With *Escort* - 4%; with *SCORE Input* - 1%]	
MusicPrinter Plus	12%
Note Processor	11%
Personal Composer	8%
THEME	6%
Encore [with *Music Time* - <1%]	3%
La mà de Guido	3%

Programs reported to be in use by less than 2% of DOS-only respondents include *COMUS*, *The Copyist*, *MusicTex*, *MidiScore*, *MidiSoft*, and *Music Tracks Pro*. Notators in the DOS world are using 1.6 programs each.

3. Software Usage on Multiple Platforms

Many users with access to multiple platforms may turn to the most hospitable environment for each new application. While we cannot produce clear evidence on this point, it is our impression that among the many respondents in this category there are three main classes: (1) those who are using Unix machines for composition and synthesis but will retreat to a Mac, PC, or Atari if they need to print common notation; (2) those who use, for example, a Mac or an Atari at home and a PC or a mainframe at work, or perhaps a portable computer of one type for home use, commuting, or research-related travel and a network of uniform machines (all Mac, all PC, all Unix) in a teaching or research setting; and (3) those who do all their computing on a local area network incorporating machines of several descriptions.

Since these users have access to a wider range of options than single-platform users, their preferences might be seen as better informed. However, commitment to any one way of generating musical notation is even lower in this group than in the others: 3.5 notation programs per user are reported! The breakdown is as follows:

Finale (Mac/Windows)	54%
SCORE (PC)	17%
Professional Composer (Mac)	16%
Notator (Atari)	11%
NoteWriter (Mac)	11%
Personal Composer (PC)	11%
Mosaic (Mac)	8%

Encore (Mac/Windows)	7%
MusicPrinter Plus (PC)	7%
CMN (Unix)	4%
Copyist (Amiga, Atari, PC)	4%
LIME (Mac)	4%
Nightingale (Mac)	4%
MusicTex (PC/Mainframe)	3%
Note Processor (PC)	3%

Programs used by less than 2% of the respondents in this group include *Berlioz*, *Deluxe Music Construction Set*, *HB Music Engraver*, *Music Time*, and *Take Control*. Several additional programs named on the questionnaire elicited no responses.

Data Formats Used for Analysis

By handling musical data as graphics and sound information, the Macintosh and Windows environments inhibit certain analytical uses of data. With regard to analytical applications, users are often limited to MIDI data, which has the significant drawback that enharmonic notations (*e.g.*, C# and Db) cannot be distinguished.

Older systems developed on mainframe computers and now operative on PCs are generally dependent on ASCII codes. (Until a few years ago all music printing programs required ASCII input.) Chief among the codes are *SCORE*, linked to one major printing program, and *DARMS*, which, in slightly varied dialects, supports several printing programs (*e.g.*, *COMUS, Muse, the Note Processor*). Of these, only the *Note Processor* is widely available at the present time. While some users find these codes clumsy to use for the purposes of generating musical notation, they may be preferable for certain kinds of academic analysis because they are significantly more articulate than MIDI data.

There are also codes that have been developed expressly for the purpose of analysis. One of these is David Huron's *Kern* representation, which is associated with a set of special Unix tools (*Humdrum*) from which highly diverse kinds of analytical routines can be assembled. We included *Kern* in our list of codes for analysis, but since the *Humdrum Toolkit* is not yet available, it was unknown to nearly all of our respondents.

Thus we report the current scope of usage of the other three codes:

MIDI	36%
DARMS	12%
SCORE	8%

Once again, platforms dictate choices, although Mac users confused us by reporting use of *DARMS* and *SCORE*. Analysts using the Mac reported as follows:

MIDI	39%
DARMS	11%
SCORE	3%

Other codes used for analysis by Mac users were *MusiCode A*, *Mustran*, *Nightingale*'s *Notelist*, and *SML* (*Structured Musical Language*), as well as undocumented custom codes. Those engaged in analysis reported using 1.4 formats each.

MIDI was also predominant on the PC but less strongly so. Analysts reported using these codes:

MIDI	24%
DARMS	15%
SCORE	14%

Also in use on the PC are Braille music notation, Finale's *Enigma* files, *Plaine and Easie*, Norbert Böker-Heil's notation metacode, and several undocumented custom schemes of representation. PC users are employing 1.8 formats for analysis.

Among those working on multiple platforms, MIDI dominates with a utilization rate of 45%. Other codes reportedly in use for analysis are:

DARMS	9%
SCORE	8%
Kern	3%

and older codes such as *OPAL* (an ancestor of *LIME*) and *Teletau*. Additionally usage of several custom codes, including one called *Sona*, was indicated.

Applications on Alternative Platforms

Twelve responses were received from persons working solely on a single platform other than a PC or Mac. The number of users is indicated in parentheses. The data provided is summarized below:

Acorn (1). This user is involved with musical notation only, using *Philip's Music Scribe*.

Amiga (2). These users are involved with sound applications and analysis using MIDI data with the *Copyist*.

Atari (5). These users are pursuing sound (MIDI), notation (*Notator*, *Score Perfect Professional*), and instructional applications.

Mainframe computers (1). This user is using *DARMS* for data management, analysis, and notation.

NeXT (1). This user is involved with both sound applications using *Csound*.

Sun workstation (2). One user is involved with notation (via *DARMS* using *MusE*). Both users are involved with analysis.

Composer and Style Preferences

What might seem the least engaging question on the survey, a rating of preferences for eight composers of the eighteenth century, elicited what were in some ways the most interesting answers. A lot of our respondents made it very clear that their preference is for music of the twentieth century. The range of tastes, as indicated by unsolicited information, was almost as broad as the contents of a music encyclopedia.

Before sharing the write-in responses, let us first give you the official answers: Mac and PC users have roughly similar tastes in music composed between 1700 and 1825 (Table 1), a period that interested CCARH in planning *MuseData* releases.

Composer	Mac Users	DOS Users	Multi-platform
Bach	42%	39%	30%
Beethoven	32%	32%	32%
Corelli	12%	19%	8%
Handel	14%	18%	9%
Haydn	16%	19%	20%
Mozart	27%	31%	22%
Telemann	13%	15%	8%
Vivaldi	11%	24%	9%

Table 1. Musical preferences by composer and platform.

When the musical terrain is expanded to include all repertories of the past two millennia, PC users appear to be somewhat more indulgent of Baroque and earlier composers than Mac users, who in the write-in portion were substantially more oriented toward later repertories (Table 2). Unix and multi-platform users like repertories with big sounds—thus orchestral music in preference to chamber or solo music. Their sympathies seem to lie mainly with nineteenth- and early-twentieth-century repertories.

The overwhelming majority of respondents supplied suggestions for additional repertories they would like to have online. Since these responses were given in a free form, they are not easily reported comparatively. Some respondents defined repertories by composer, some by time period, some by place, and some by musical genre. Some were clearly thinking of written scores, while others were clearly thinking of sound information divorced from a written score. In the revised questionnaire, we defined a number of specific categories by time and genre, thereby gaining a more easily managed set of responses. Since some users made multiple suggestions relating to a single category, however, we cannot provide percentages in Table 2.

Repertory	Mac Users	DOS Users	Multi-platform
Plainchant	6	4	5
Medieval	8	3	4
Renaissance	23	14	10
17th-century instrumental	9	3	3
18th-century, other composers	2	3	
19th-century instrumental	21	10	9
19th-century vocal	12	3	10
early 20th-century	41	11	26
post 1950	9	13	3

Table 2. Musical preferences by period, genre, and platform.

Specific composer indications were as follows:

Alkan-1	Dalla Vecchia-1	Mahler-2	Schoenberg-8
Babbitt-2	Debussy-4	Messaien-1	Shostakovich-1
Bartók-6	Dufay-2	Milhaud-1	Stockhausen-1
Belet-1	Dvořák-1	Morricone-1	Stravinsky-11
Berg-3	Ellington-1	Musorgsky-1	Strauss, R.-1
Berlioz-1	Falla-1	Ockeghem-1	Varese-1
Bernstein-1	Hasse-1	Pachelbel-1	Vaughan-
Billings-1	Heiller-1	Paganini-1	Williams-1
Boulez-1	Hindemith-1	Palestrina-3	Verdi-2
Brahms-4	Ives-1	Puccini-2	Vitry-1
Britten-1	Janaček-1	Rameau-2	Wagner-2
Brubeck-1	Josquin-2	Ravel-4	Webern-4
Carter-1	Lassus-1	Reger-1	
Chopin-3	Lutosławski-1	Scarlatti, A.-1	
Copland-2	Machaut-2	Schubert-3	

Generic requests mentioned jazz (4), wind band music (1), American folk songs (1), and ethnic repertories from India (2), Indonesia (2), China (1), Japan (1), Ethiopia (1), Ghana (1), India (1), and North Africa (2) as well as non-Western repertories in general (3) and music in which "the pitches are not quantized" (1).

Copyright Issues Relating to the Use of Musical Data

In judging the feasibility of these highly diverse repertories it is necessary to take into account the fact that jazz and many other ethnic repertories based on oral tradition require the representation of recorded rather than notated information. Conversion of actual performance to files useful for study and analysis is a non-trivial task to which research has been devoted sporadically for 15 or so years.

Much of the music of the twentieth century is protected by copyright, which strictly prohibits redistribution in any form except with written permission. Statutes, which vary by country, can pertain for as long as 75 years after the death of the composer. Only recently have the last of the protected works of Ravel, for example, entered the public domain.

Copyright questions also plague efforts to convert the informational content of phonorecords to machine-readable files. In traditional legal thought, a written score was usually taken to contain the primary version of a work. Performances and recordings were viewed as derivatives. To prospective users, electronic materials may be especially desirable when no written score was ever published, but if no score was published, it may be especially difficult to trace current copyright owners and/or to establish the availability of the hypothetical "written works" underlying recorded performances.

The computer is playing a central role in reconstituting the relationship among different kinds of copyright. Increasingly, electronic files rather than written scores contain the primary versions of new works. The idea of a necessary order of things—first the score, then the performance, then the recording—is giving way to the recognition that a machine-readable file can be converted for use in diverse applications among which there is no necessary order. More problemmatical is the fact that works that exist in machine-readable form are always potentially dynamic, and exact details may change from moment to moment.

Much of the music being composed now will not suffer the same isolation from electronic access as music of the past because it may first exist as a computer-readable file. Composers of the present and editors of music of the past must decide for themselves whether, and under what circumstances, the electronic version of their works should be made available for academic use. Despite the fact that it will not go away, this important issue continues to receive less attention than it deserves in scholarly circles.

Sources of Information about Music Software

In the questionnaire that was distributed electronically, we asked respondents to rate sources of information about music software. The overwhelming preference, on the basis of accuracy and reliability, is for the non-promotional written word, especially as found in academic journals and academic newsgroups.

Source	Favorable	Unfavorable
Network newsgroups and bulletin boards	14	1
Academic newsgroups	20	1
Commercial/trade journals	14	3
Academic journals	20	1
Computer hardware vendors	8	6
Computer software vendors	3	5
Music software vendors	4	4
Music hardware vendors	2	7
Trade fairs	1	8
Promotional literature	6	6
Newspapers reviews of software	3	7
Television reviews of software	0	3
Video presentations	1	4

Data Use

One further question probed possible formats for distribution of musical data. A preference for greater quantities on fewer storage media was clearly expressed, although we detected a distinct difference between those answering on their own behalf and those replying on behalf of institutions: individuals prefer diskettes; institutions prefer CD ROMS. Some respondents did not answer this question, while others gave multiple answers. It appears that preference may be colored by platform use: at the present time CD ROMS seem to be more widely in use by Mac users than by PC users. Many Unix systems have no provision for diskettes and must turn to networks or CD ROMs for data distribution.

Distribution format	Mac	PC	Multi-platform
Single orders, one work per diskette	18%	13%	14%
Single orders, multiple works per diskette	40%	38%	30%
Subscription, one work per diskette	5%	0%	4%
Subscription, multiple works per diskette	10%	3%	9%
Subscription, single-composer CD ROMS	40%	14%	28%
Subscription, single-genre CD ROMS	0%	1%	0%

Several respondents suggested FTP and listservers as means of data distribution. Even if copyright and data integrity were not issues, incompatible formats would thwart efforts at widespread distribution, since at the present time most musical data files are software-specific.

CCARH extends its special thanks to all respondents and questionnaire distributors for their cooperation in this survey. Responses were compiled by Nancy Solomon.

Index

All submissions should be made both in hardcopy, following the indications given below, and on a 3.5"/1.44 MB diskette, with fonts stripped unless the text was prepared using *WordPerfect*.

Italics: Please italicize titles of books, journals, and proceedings; titles of major texted musical works, such as operas; e-mail addresses, names of computer directories and files, and titles of programs and specific versions of computer languages (*e.g.*, *Turbo Pascal*) but not of languages (Pascal) or operating systems (Unix). Instructions to be entered on a computer screen by the user should be in **bold face**.

Titles: Titles of articles within books or journals, of short texted musical works, such as songs, and of nicknames for musical works (*e.g.*, "Moonlight" Sonata) should be placed within double quotation marks. For titles in English, the main words should begin with a capital letter. Titles in other languages follow native style.

Names: In bibliographical references, please include first names of authors and editors as well as volume/issue numbers (in Arabic numerals) and page numbers of articles in journals and collected writings. Please observe the name order indicated below.

(1) Single author, book:
> Mazzola, Guerino. *Geometrie der Töne*. Basel: Birkhäuser, 1990.

(2) Single author, article in journal:
> Bel, Bernard. "Time in Musical Structures," *Interface,* 19/2-3 (1990), 107-135.

(3) Single author, article in book or proceedings:
> Morehen, John. "Byrd's Manuscript Motets: A New Perspective" in *Byrd Studies*, ed. Alan Brown and Richard Turbut (Cambridge: Cambridge University Press, 1991), pp. 51-62.

(4) Single author, thesis or dissertation:
> Diener, Glendon R. "Modeling Music Notation: A Three-Dimensional Approach." Ph.D. Thesis, Stanford University, 1991.

(5) Multiple authors, article in journal:
> Hill, John Walter, and Tom Ward. "Two Relational Databases for Finding Text Paraphrases in Musicological Research," *Computers and the Humanities*, 23/4 (1989), 105-111.

Bibliographical listings, which should be limited to eight items, should be given in alphabetical order of the authors' surnames. Multiple references by the same author should be given alphabetically by title.

Citations within the main text may give the author and the year only, *e.g.* "(Hill 1989)". If multiple writings by the same author occur in the same year, please append designations (Hill 1989a, Hill 1989b, etc.) to appropriate bibliographical citations in the references.